Suggestions for

Set aside a regular time and plac[e]
and pray undisturbed. Before yo[u]
it helpful, use the BRF prayer on

In *Guidelines*, the introductory
themes to be studied, while the units of comment can be used daily, weekly or
whatever best fits your timetable. You will need a Bible (more than one if you
want to compare different translations) as Bible passages are not included.
Please don't be tempted to skip the Bible reading because you know the
passage well. We will have utterly failed if we don't bring our readers into
engagement with the word of God. At the end of each week is a 'Guidelines'
section, offering further thoughts about, or practical application of, what
you have been studying.

Occasionally, you may read something in *Guidelines* that you find particularly challenging, even uncomfortable. This is inevitable in a series of
notes which draws on a wide spectrum of contributors and doesn't believe
in ducking difficult issues. Indeed, we believe that *Guidelines* readers much
prefer thought-provoking material to a bland diet that only confirms what
they already think.

If you do disagree with a contributor, you may find it helpful to go through
these three steps. First, think about why you feel uncomfortable. Perhaps this
is an idea that is new to you, or you are not happy about the way something
has been expressed. Or there may be something more substantial – you
may feel that the writer is guilty of sweeping generalisation, factual error, or
theological or ethical misjudgement. Second, pray that God would use this
disagreement to teach you more about his word and about yourself. Third,
have a deeper read about the issue. There are further reading suggestions
at the end of each writer's block of notes. And then, do feel free to write to
the contributor or the editor of *Guidelines*. We welcome communication,
by email, phone or letter, as it enables us to discover what has been useful,
challenging or infuriating for our readers. We don't always promise to change
things, but we will always listen and think about your ideas, complaints or
suggestions. Thank you!

To send feedback, please email **enquiries@brf.org.uk**, phone **+44 (0)1865
319700** or write to the address shown opposite.

Writers in this issue

Bill Goodman encourages and enables lifelong learning in the Anglican diocese of Sheffield. He's also written Advent and Lent courses (available at **lightsforchrist.uk**).

Peter Hatton is a former tutor at Bristol Baptist College, where he taught after 25 years in Methodist pastoral ministry. Preaching, some writing projects and looking after grandchildren are keeping him occupied in 'retirement'.

Richard Martin served with the Church Army before ordination to a curacy and an incumbency in Gravesend. He is now priest-in-charge of three parishes in the Gloucester diocese and is a Third Order Franciscan.

Ruth Bancewicz is church engagement director at The Faraday Institute for Science and Religion, Cambridge. The other contributors are former Faraday staff or have worked closely with The Faraday Institute.

Andy Angel is the director of formation for ministry in the diocese of Oxford, having recently been a vicar and previously having taught in two Anglican training colleges.

Helen Miller is head of Postgraduate Studies at Moorlands College and lectures on the college's MA and BA Applied Theology programmes.

Stephen Finamore is a minister of the Baptist Union of Great Britain and former principal at Bristol Baptist College. He is the author of *Romans Unwrapped*, which can be found on the BRF Resource Hub.

David Spriggs is a Baptist minister who served in three pastorates before working for the Evangelical Alliance and Bible Society. Since his retirement he has fulfilled part-time posts with three churches.

Karen O'Donnell is a trauma theologian. She has published widely on this topic including, most recently, *The Dark Womb: Re-conceiving theology through reproductive loss* (SCM Press, 2022). She is the director of studies at Westcott House, Cambridge.

Isabelle Hamley is a theologian, writer and broadcaster, currently working as theological adviser to the Church of England's House of Bishops. She has previously held posts as a university chaplain, parish priest, tutor in Old Testament and chaplain to the Archbishop of Canterbury.

Leoné Martin is an associate pastor at Cannon Street Memorial Baptist Church. She is passionate about equipping Christians for every good work through her teaching and writing, and is currently completing a theology research masters at Bristol Baptist College.

The editors write...

This issue of *Guidelines* brings us a feast of good things as we start the journey towards Advent and Christmas.

Our Advent series will get underway with David Spriggs, as he takes a look at the biblical witness to John the Baptist, whose extraordinary birth preceded Jesus'. Taking us up to Christmas Day, Isabelle Hamley will encourage us to think about Advent and the art of waiting, showing how different biblical characters embodied this act of waiting throughout history.

We continue a number of our series, too. Stephen Finamore rounds off his four-part series on Romans with 'Riding with Romans', which takes us through the final three chapters of the book. Andy Angel also closes out his series on Matthew as we experience once again Jesus' death, resurrection and commission to his disciples. Bill Goodman will continue with Book 2 of the Psalms (42—72), investigating God's message to the world.

Our Old Testament series for this issue is on Proverbs, with Peter Hatton unpacking this book which is sometimes accused of putting forward 'a complacent, self-satisfied morality'; instead, Peter shows us how the first nine chapters of Proverbs teach us much, especially in our 'beautiful but troubled' world. Meanwhile Leoné Martin, a new contributor, takes a deep dive into the famous John 15 passage in which Jesus gives us the beautiful metaphor of the 'true vine'.

Helen Miller (née Morris) brings us a fascinating series on images of the church in the New Testament, while Richard Martin explores Francistide to coincide with the Feast of St Francis at the beginning of October. New writer Karen O'Donnell brings us a week of notes on reading the Bible through the lens of trauma. Finally, Ruth Bancewicz and her team of scientists, who previously wrote about creation in *Guidelines*, return with a bioethical toolkit to help us think about how biblical principles apply to a Christian understanding of bioethics.

We hope this has whetted your appetite! May God bless your reading and reflections.

Rachel Tranter and Olivia Warburton

The BRF Prayer

Faithful God,
thank you for growing BRF
from small beginnings
into a worldwide family of ministries.
We rejoice as young and old
discover you through your word
and grow daily in faith and love.
Keep us humble in your service,
ambitious for your glory
and open to new opportunities.
For your name's sake,
Amen.

Psalms Book II (Psalms 42—72): prayers of David and others – God's message for the world

Bill Goodman

In Book 1 (Psalms 1—41), we noticed the frequent references to King David, particularly in the headings (superscriptions) with which many psalms begin. These could indicate psalms written by David, or could mean 'to/for David', 'about David' or 'on behalf of David'. They might also refer to one of the subsequent kings who followed after David in his family line.

But although King David earned the accolade 'Israel's singer of songs' (2 Samuel 23:1; this is often translated differently), he was not the only composer whose songs came to be cherished and preserved. Book 2 of the Psalter begins with a collection connected with 'the sons of Korah' (Psalms 42—49). They seem to have been a group of worship leaders in the Jerusalem temple, part of the tribe of Levi (glimpsed in 2 Chronicles 20:19). Another worship leader appointed by David was Asaph (1 Chronicles 16:7 – see Psalm 50); and Book 2 closes with a glimpse of David's successor in a psalm entitled 'Solomon's' (Psalm 72).

All the psalms in Book 1 spoke directly to or else about Yhwh (translated as 'LORD' in most English versions), the particular divine name revealed to Israel through Moses. In Book 2 this suddenly changes: many of these psalms prefer to use 'Elohim', the more general word for God. Might this be a collection of psalms from a conservative group, wary of using the divine name in case they take it in vain? Book 2 also refers far more than Book 1 to 'the nations', 'foreigners', 'all humankind' and 'the ends of the earth'. And these non-Israelite peoples are not just spoken about but addressed directly, inviting them to turn to Israel's God and challenging them to walk in God's ways. Might this be why these psalms prefer to proclaim 'Elohim' – a more inclusive term for God that will sound less parochial and resonate with this wider audience? We cannot say for sure.

The voice of lament, which we heard repeatedly in Book 1, becomes even more prominent in Book 2. We also hear increasing mention of Zion, the hill which became the focal point of Israel's worship from King David's time onwards. Zion becomes a reminder of the presence, holiness and accessibility of Israel's God; as ever, it is to this God above all that the psalms direct our attention.

Unless otherwise stated, Bible quotations are taken from the NRSV.

1 Giving your *nephesh* a good talking to

Psalms 42—43

Book 1 began with a striking, comforting image: the godly person as a flourishing, well-watered tree planted alongside streams (1:3). Book 2 begins with an equally vivid image, but this one is disturbing: the godly person pictured as a deer, not flourishing but parched with thirst (42:1). A desperate longing to draw close to the living God is overwhelming the speaker, bringing a crushing sense of desolation – for God seems a long way off. Water is essential, to nourish and bring life; but here its dangers are evoked, with the image of an overwhelming flood – sent or permitted by God (42:7).

In Psalms 42—43 (the structure and symmetry of these two psalms confirm Jewish tradition that we should read them as one whole), the word *nephesh* appears seven times (42:1, 2, 4, 5, 6, 11; 43:5). It refers not simply to an internal 'soul' (as English translations often render it), but to the whole life of a person, the self, including their body and desires. The speaker seems to be a worship leader who longs to go physically to a place (presumably the Jerusalem temple) where God can be encountered afresh (42:4).

Unusually, this psalm is addressed repeatedly to self, rather than to God. Three times we overhear an internal argument, as it asks: 'Why are you cast down, O my *nephesh*, and why are you disquieted within me?' (42:5, 11; 43:5). Encouragement to keep hoping in God is needed, particularly when facing hostility from others (42:9–10). Sometimes that encouragement comes from other people, but here the speaker takes personal responsibility for it, exhorting self (*nephesh*) to keep waiting with expectant hope for God to intervene and do what is needed.

In this psalm, God seems absent – yet turns out to be constantly present, mentioned no less than 22 times in phrases suggesting close relationship, as 'the living God', 'your God', 'my God', 'my living God', 'my rock', 'God my exceeding joy'. At the very centre of the psalm (42:8) is its only mention of Yhwh, who is the source of divine loving-kindness, by day and night. A promise to praise 'my help and my God' is given the final word (43:5). God's goodness and commitment is declared in this psalm, even while God's response to the immediate need is still awaited and longed for.

2 Not guilty! Not fair, God!

Psalm 44

In Psalms 42—43 we heard challenging questions addressed to the self; in this next psalm we hear even more challenging questions – addressed to God.

Up to now in the Psalter we have repeatedly heard the voice of the individual speaking to and about God. Now, for the first time, that 'I' is replaced by 'we': the community speaks. Yet interwoven with this communal voice is still a singular one (vv. 4, 6, 15–16): perhaps the king, or a prophet or worship leader. We get the sense of a liturgy, with the voice of the leader occasionally heard while the voice of the congregation predominates.

In response to some recent disaster involving military defeat (vv. 9–11), the people pour out their pain and anger together, expressing it directly to God. God is their ultimate king (v. 5) and therefore commander-in-chief held responsible for the defeat in battle. They are convinced that God is mighty, just and committed to them. Yet they cannot square this understanding of who God is and how God acts with their recent experience; tension between the two is bewildering and intensely painful. Their complaint accuses God of being the problem – even while their praying suggests that God is also the solution!

The people begin by reminding God of the commitment and help which God gave to Israel so long ago, contrasting this with their present devastation – and then they accuse, calling God to account for not keeping God's promises. They are convinced of their own innocence: not a claim to be perfect, but an insistence that they have not broken their side of the covenant agreement and therefore that God has no reason to punish them for breaking it. (Josiah's death in battle, after his renewal of the covenant, might be one possible setting for this psalm; see 2 Kings 23.) They plead with God in urgent imperatives, to wake up, to get up, to redeem (similar phrases can be found in Psalms 7:6; 35:23; 78:65). The basis of the plea is simply *khesed*, God's faithful commitment – this psalm's final word.

This prayer expresses assertiveness – some might say impertinence, perhaps even arrogance! Its inclusion in the Psalter is a challenge: how honest and bold do we dare to be in our prayers?

3 God's king and queen

Psalm 45

The Psalter keeps surprising us. In contrast to the agonising of the previous psalms, we now find one which is thoroughly upbeat, titled 'A love song'. This psalm is not addressed to God, but to Israel's king and his bride, which suggests that it was composed for a royal wedding or similar, with these words from a court poet providing the equivalent of the best man's speech!

In verse 6, the divine and human seem to blur together, with their thrones apparently fusing into one. Who is being addressed here? Is this a liturgy, with the worship leader at this point turning to God? Or is the king actually being proclaimed as divine? Some nearby nations used to do this, but Israel avoided adopting this kind of idolatry, allowing prophets to challenge the authority of kings. So a better translation may be: 'Your throne is God's forever and ever.' The human king is reminded that he rules on God's behalf, not simply in his own authority, as we saw in Psalm 2; it is God who has anointed him (v. 7). No mention is made of conquering new territories; rather than building his own empire, he is to fight God's battles, for truth and justice (v. 4)

Royal marriages have often been used to strengthen alliances between powerful dynasties, and this kind of power politics may be in play here. The surprising mention of Tyre (v. 12) in the rather stern words addressed to the bride evoke the image of Jezebel, a princess from that neighbouring kingdom who married Israel's King Ahab (1 Kings 16:29–34). Ahab, like Solomon before him (1 Kings 11:1–8), became infamous for apparently allowing a foreign queen to lead him and his people into idolatry. Like Elijah to Ahab, this psalm warns Israel and its kings against unfaithfulness; any new queen must follow the example of Ruth ('Your people shall be my people, and your God my God', Ruth 1:16), not Jezebel.

After Israel's monarchy ended, this psalm was interpreted to represent the marriage of God's Messiah and the people of God, an idea which Christians adopted, seeing Jesus as the truly divine king (Hebrews 1:8–9). It may also have been used by ordinary couples on their wedding days, depicting them as king and queen for a day.

4 A mighty fortress

In Psalm 45 we witnessed a royal wedding, suggesting potential for a Davidic dynasty continuing into the future. But what does that future look like for Israel and its kings? Can this small nation really thrive in the turbulent world that surrounds it? These next three psalms give the answer, proclaiming promises of hope. Israel can navigate that world and find security in her God, who reigns in the iconic city of Jerusalem.

That 'city of God', glimpsed in 46:4–5, comes more strongly into focus in Psalm 48, which identifies it as Zion (the hill on which Jerusalem was built). Zion's towers, ramparts and citadels proclaim its security. The temptation may be simply to rely on those human constructions; the calling is to see them as expressions of the invincibility of the divine king who is enthroned at the heart of the city. That is what makes God's holy hill (which is actually not exceptionally high or striking to look at) genuinely beautiful and formidable. It is in God that people can find their true refuge and strength (46:1) and experience God's steadfast love as they worship (48:9).

Who is this awesome divine king? Another feature of these three psalms is the unexpected reappearance of the divine name Yhwh (LORD), which Book 2 of the Psalms generally avoids using, preferring simply Elohim (God). Yhwh, the God of Jacob, is the God of armies who is 'with us' (46:7, 11; 48:8); the God of Abraham, Yhwh Most High, is the great king over all the earth (47:2, 5, 9) who dwells on Mount Zion (48:1). Using imagery similar to other ancient accounts of Babylon's chief god Marduk and the Canaanite storm god Baal, these psalms appropriate and challenge those accounts – proclaiming that Yhwh is the true God, not any of those others. And Yhwh is not simply concerned about one chosen people; all peoples and nations are invited and challenged to join in the worship of Israel's God (47:1–2, 7–9).

These three psalms speak about and to God. But at one point, suddenly and unexpectedly, God speaks, commanding humanity to 'be still, and know that I am God' (46:10). Our human tendency is to strive, often resulting in violent conflict and destruction; our calling is to find our defence and destiny by stopping, looking to God and allowing God to rule.

5 Have mercy on me

A few psalms focus on the speaker's sense of sin; in this one we hear words of confession and pleas for forgiveness. Yet Psalm 51 begins with grace: before any mention of sin, the opening verse focuses on God's abundant mercy and steadfast love, using words that famously describe Yhwh's own character in Exodus 34:6–7. The radical nature of God's grace becomes even more striking if we read this psalm, as its heading invites us to, in the light of the story of King David when he was confronted by the prophet Nathan over his abuse of Bathsheba and Uriah (2 Samuel 11:1—12:15). In that account we see King David breaking five of the ten commandments, with hugely destructive consequences to others and to himself – yet still finding forgiveness!

The honesty in this psalm is striking; the speaker's relationship with God is open, holding nothing back. There is no attempt at self-justification, nor is God accused and blamed, as we saw in Psalm 44. In this particular case, responsibility for what has gone wrong is taken clearly and wholly on the self. Yielding that self, allowing the willpower to be broken and the heart to be remade, is what is needed (vv. 10, 16–17).

With that honesty comes an intensity in the words expressed, with a degree of hyperbole. Does the speaker actually think that one's sins only affect God and not our neighbours (v. 4)? Or that sex is somehow sinful and his parents are to blame (v. 5)? It makes far more sense to hear passionate exaggeration here, a conviction that sin is an all-pervading reality which none of us can avoid or escape – and which really matters to God, not just to us. Intensity also comes across in the stream of imperatives which abound in this psalm (look at vv. 1–2, 6–12, 14–15, 18). In these we hear strong, urgent pleas for God to respond to the felt need and bring life-restoring action.

As the psalm progresses, the speaker seems to go through a transition: the strong sense of awareness of personal sin in the opening part gradually diminishes, replaced by increasing awareness of God. With this comes a desire to respond to God's grace, by sharing what has been learned with others (vv. 6, 13) and giving praise to God (vv. 14–15), growing into a humble and genuine worshipper (vv. 16–19).

6 Betrayed and devastated

Confusion, painful chaos, life unravelling: this psalm expresses those feelings, not just in what it says but also in the way it is written. The medium underlines the message: it seems uneven, disjointed – erratic in focus, tenses and grammar, with meaning sometimes uncertain. It conveys the sense of an emotional roller-coaster and the wildly fluctuating mixture of thoughts from someone experiencing deep trauma.

Enemies abound, expressed as plural. But then suddenly the focus shifts to a particular individual (vv. 13–14, 20–21). Is the individual betrayer part of that larger group of enemies? Or does one bring reminders of the other? The two seem to blur together in the ebb and flow of grief and anger. The speaker comes across as an isolated individual, speaking of 'I' and 'me'; only once does this expand to 'we', in a wistful memory, grieving over the loss of former companionship and fellowship (v. 14).

The pain has physical dimensions (v. 4) prompted by emotional violation. The betrayer was not a passing acquaintance but someone close and trusted. A relationship so intimate, so sacred that it was understood as a 'covenant', has been violated by this deceptive smooth-talker (vv. 20–21); trust has been shattered.

Different responses well up. One is a longing to escape from it all to a safe place and rest there (vv. 6–8). Another is wishing suffering and death on these enemies (vv. 15, 23). This kind of verbal violence, asking God to punish those who deserve it, gives the angry sufferer an alternative to taking the matter into their own hands in a violent way.

A theme in this group of psalms (Psalms 54—59) is trust. The closing section of this one (vv. 16–23) presents a challenge: to keep trusting in God. The sufferer urges people (or perhaps self) to 'cast your burden on Yhwh' and find security there (v. 22). The crisis and trauma are not resolved, but the invitation to throw on to God what other people throw on to us brings some hope.

The heading 'of David' might remind us of times when he was pursued by King Saul or his own son Absalom. Some recent commentators enlarge the picture, imagining Psalm 55 on the lips of David's daughter Tamar, protesting at her experience of being raped by David's favourite son (2 Samuel 13:1–20).

Guidelines

- In addition to King David, the Psalter embraces other figures as sources or inspirations in its songs and prayers, such as the 'Korahites' (Psalms 42—49). Which prayer and song writers do you and your church draw on today, to nourish your prayer life and worship? Is there a diverse and enriching blend? Or might you include some other voices?

- Psalms 42 and 46 both provide contrasting images of water: life-giving streams and also life-threatening floods. A sense of threat from the world around us can easily induce anxiety; yet, at the same time, we can find security in God who preserves us, even in the midst of turmoil. Does this resonate with your own experience, either now or in the past?

- The psalms we have looked at also give us contrasting pictures of the city: as a safe place of refuge with God at the heart of it (48:1–3) or as a place of violence and iniquity, with oppression and fraud in the public square (55:9–11). With these contrasts in mind, pray for urban areas you know and those who share Christ's love in them. Pray also for countries facing unrest or oppression.

- The directness and honesty of these psalms is striking – challenging self (Psalms 42—43), blaming God for rejecting God's people (Psalm 44), proclaiming God's protection of those people (Psalms 46—48), blaming self for sin and pleading for mercy (Psalm 51), protesting against the sin of an abuser (Psalm 55). Are you able to pray with this kind of honesty and directness? What about your church?

- Some readers propose that we hear Psalm 55 as the lament of a woman who has suffered sexual violence. Some churches take up this psalm to express their corporate experience of being persecuted for their faith. Laments such as this give back speech to those who have been robbed of it, enabling them to articulate and protest at their violation. They can also help the rest of us to support and pray for people suffering in these ways. Consider how you might do this in your context.

1 Sheltering, awakening, singing

Psalm 57

In Psalm 57 and its immediate neighbours, we find pleas for God's help along with encouragement to trust God in all circumstances. The opening of this particular psalm reminds us of David, hiding from Saul into a cave (see 1 Samuel 24), to indicate the kind of circumstance in which it might be prayed.

Good things are worth relishing, treasuring and repeating. Those who wrote the psalms seem to have treasured particular phrases and recycled them. Thus verse 10 is almost identical to Psalm 36:5; while the closing section of Psalm 57 is identical with the opening verses of Psalm 108 (a psalm which also has verses in common with Psalm 60). In addition, Psalm 57 echoes a lot of the language of its immediate predecessor, Psalm 56, from the identical opening plea onwards.

The psalmists were also happy to mix different moods and genres, as we see in the two distinct halves of Psalm 57. Lament and desperation (vv. 1–4, 6) give way to trusting and praising God (vv. 5, 7–11). Yet there is no obvious sign of improvement in the speaker's circumstances. Time seems to collapse, with future events referred to in the present tense: God's saving action has not yet arrived, but somehow is experienced in the 'here and now'. Even while destruction is rampaging all around, the speaker can find refuge under the wings of God Most High. This beautiful image (v. 1; see also 61:4, 63:7) might refer to the winged figures of the cherubim on top of the ark of the covenant, suggesting a worshipper in the temple. Or it might be a more general picture of God as a mother bird, gathering and protecting her young when danger threatens.

Another intriguing image is the urgent need to wake up. The speaker feels a desire to wake self, wake musical instruments – even wake the dawn (v. 8). This urge to sing, a night-time eagerness to praise God, is so strong that it cannot wait for sunrise. While normally dawn would be expected to wake people, this David is already awake at night and wanting to rouse the dawn! This eagerness to praise involves giving witness among different peoples and nations – particularly to what God is going to do in future.

2 Embodied life in its fullness

Psalm 63

If time allows, read Psalms 61—63 together. Look out for images and themes they share, particularly their call to trust in God's protection during scary times and situations.

The word *nephesh*, which we noticed in Psalms 42—43, reappears in Psalm 63, occurring four times, notably at the beginning of each major section (vv. 1, 5, 9; also at the end of the central section, v. 8). As we saw earlier, 'soul' is too insubstantial and misleading as a translation; *nephesh* is about a person's whole life and longings – not some disembodied soul, but an embodied person. The one who thirsts for God has a body of flesh which aches for God (v. 1).

As if to underline this, images of bodily life abound in this psalm: we are shown hands raised in prayer to God and holding tight to a loved one in committed, intimate embrace (vv. 4, 8), eyes that somehow see God's presence, power and glory (v. 2), the body of the speaker lying in bed with a mind that seeks to understand God's ways (v. 6). Repeatedly we glimpse the mouth: at one time, dry and desperately thirsty (v. 1); at another, feasting hungrily on God's grace and then responding with thankful praise, calling and singing out to God (vv. 3–5). In the final verse, these images of the mouth multiply: the king rejoices in God, the faithful swear oaths in God's name – and in contrast, the mouths of lying enemies are silenced (v. 11).

We also find striking pictures of security in relationship with God. The speaker clings to God (v. 8) – the same word used elsewhere to express the bond between husband and wife (Genesis 2:24) and also the covenant bond between Yhwh and Israel (Deuteronomy 10:20; 11:22; 30:20). Shelter can be found under God's wings, that striking image we also noticed in yesterday's psalm (v. 7; compare 57:1, 61:4). The presence of God is close and protective, as it was for David during times in the wilderness.

Living embodied life in all its fullness involves longing, trusting and delighting in the presence of God, despite ongoing challenges and pressures from hostile people. Discovering God's committed, steadfast love is more precious than anything else, even the gift of life itself (v. 3).

3 The blessed become channels of blessing

Psalm 67

Psalms 65—67 share certain themes: you might like to read all three of these psalms together, looking out for mention of harvest, blessing and God's commitment to all peoples.

One of the Bible's powerful, recurring messages is that God's blessing is given to a particular people, so that through them it may then be shared with the wider world (vv. 1–3). God promised to Abram that 'in you all the families of the earth shall be blessed' (Genesis 12:3). As the story unfolded, God gave Israel a priestly role, to convey divine blessing among the nations (Exodus 19:6).

Psalm 67 explores that promise to Abram, seen through the lens of another text found later in the Torah: the priestly blessing proclaimed by Aaron and his sons (Numbers 6:24–26). While that blessing was addressed to 'you', this psalm changes the wording to 'us': so now the wider circle of worshippers can use these words to pray God's blessing on one another. While Aaron's blessing focused on Israel, Psalm 67 widens the focus, with that blessing on Israel intended to flow out from Israel and benefit the whole world. While Aaron's blessing repeatedly used the divine name Yhwh, this psalm never mentions that specific name of Israel's God; it alludes to Yhwh ('God, our God', v. 6), but chooses instead the more general term for God ('Elohim').

So this psalm develops the Aaronic blessing in ways that highlight God's commitment to the whole world. All the nations can know and worship Israel's God – a message emphasised by repetition (vv. 3, 5). Set between those two verses, the central words at the heart of the psalm affirm that this same God guides all the nations, not simply Israel; and decides for all people, not just for Israel – and does so fairly (v. 4).

Having begun with blessing, the psalm also ends with it (vv. 6–7). One practical manifestation of that blessing is a good harvest (v. 6): blessing is not just some vague sense of spiritual well-being, but is also seen in practical, physical experiences. The life-giving sunshine which ripens crops can be a reminder of God's warming presence, described earlier as God's face, shining towards the psalmist, imparting life (v. 1; see also 4:6; 31:16; 42:2; 119:135). Perhaps this group of psalms (Psalms 65—67) was used by Israel in harvest celebrations.

4 Almost drowning

Pleas, complaints, confession, prayers for punishment, praise – all these are found in this one long psalm. Complaint is the voice that predominates, making itself heard three times (vv. 1–4, 7–12, 19–21). False accusations of theft, ridicule for devotion to God, experiencing taunts and isolation – all these experiences contribute to a sense of drowning in deep waters, which are often a symbol for chaotic and dangerous forces in biblical writings (vv. 1–2, 14–15). Yet, as we have seen in other laments, the psalmist suddenly turns to praise at the end. Is this in response to receiving a word of encouragement? Or an improvement in circumstances? Or else simply in faith that the grim situation will change for the better?

We don't know what prompted the writing of this psalm, entitled simply 'of David'. We do know that various faithful servants of God down the years, trying to make sense of their suffering, have found resources in it. Along with Psalm 22, this is the psalm most quoted and alluded to in the New Testament. All four gospel writers refer to verse 21 (Mark 15:36; Matthew 27:34, 48; Luke 23:36; John 19:29–30). Jesus interprets his experience of being hated in light of verse 4 (John 15:25). Verse 9 helped early Christians understand Jesus' violent action in the temple, as well as other people's violence against Jesus and against them (John 2:17; Romans 15:3). Paul also sees his own people experiencing the blindness and retribution which verses 22–23 calls for (Romans 11:9–10).

Intriguingly, the part of Psalm 69 which New Testament writers draw on most is the part some of us might draw back from – where the speaker calls for God's anger and action against the enemies who are causing such torment (vv. 22–29). These verses are praying for God's will to be done on earth, with conviction that wrongdoing should receive its just reward. Psalm 69 and other psalms like it protest against injustice, while letting go of the temptation to respond to violence with counter-violence – that responsibility is placed into God's hands.

As he hangs on the cross, Jesus turns to psalms he has memorised (Psalms 22:1; 31:5) – but does not pray words from psalms demanding divine vengeance. His challenge to love and pray for our enemies is another core part of our Christian calling (Matthew 5:43–48), alongside his call to strive for God's just reign in our world (Matthew 6:10, 33).

5 Continuing faithfully to the end

We're all getting older; it's a universal experience. Psalm 71 reflects this experience, as part of its response to a time of crisis (no person or incident is named at the start). This anonymous psalm gives us glimpses of someone seeking to grow old with grace – God's grace.

The speaker remembers encounters with God in much earlier years, as a young person; listening to that younger self seems to help rejuvenate the spirit. It prompts more reflections, going back beyond the limits of memory, to the very earliest moments; with this comes a glimpse of God as a caring midwife, present and intimately involved even from the beginning of life (v. 5–6).

We return to the present moment. The psalmist considers the prospect (or perhaps current experience) of growing old, with honesty about the anxieties still to be faced (vv. 9–11, 18). No comfortable retirement here: there are enemies pressing in, making the future uncertain and daunting. Yet there is no sense of a desire to wallow in nostalgia; the focus remains forward-looking, willing and eager to be open to God's future. Part of the secret is consciously redirecting attention away from self and towards God (notice how many times the words 'you' or 'your' appear in the opening and closing verses).

Present experience blurs into tomorrow and the days beyond it, in the repeated use of *tāmid*, meaning 'continually' or 'always'. The psalm speaks of continually coming to God, the source of strength and security (v. 3). Praise is also continual, an ongoing way of life (v. 6). And the speaker's hope is continual, in spite of life's crises and threats, prompting further praise and witness day by day (vv. 14–15). In this steady perseverance, we see spiritual vitality continuing, throughout life and on into old age – refreshed by God's continual acts of faithfulness. That prompts a longing to share God's grace with the next generation (vv. 17–18), so that younger voices will energise and rejuvenate the community of worshippers once more.

Joyful praise and testimony have the final word, in the closing verses, along with continued trust in God's help and protection (vv. 22–24). Worship, witness, continuing discipleship – there is still so much to be done, in however many days and years remain!

6 Giving the king a job description

Challenging the powerful can be done in different ways. For the direct approach, see Psalm 52; a more indirect approach is found in Psalm 72. At first sight, this psalm might seem obsequious and obnoxious: the fawning flattery of a courtier eager to please the master by singing his praises. But on closer examination, the psalm proves more subtle and distinctly subversive: it is, in effect, giving the king a job description!

The speaker proclaims that anyone ruling God's people must resist the temptation to be self-serving and exploitative; instead, the king's calling is to protect the vulnerable, judge with justice and bring prosperity to all the people, not just to himself (vv. 2–4; compare Psalm 45:4). This king is to have compassion on the weak and needy, using his power to rescue them from oppression; the impact is like life-giving rain, refreshing the land (v. 6). Royal power is to be used in serving the powerless among his subjects; a radically different approach to the pattern of many absolute monarchies, in those days and in more recent times.

Here is a noble vision for David's successors, beginning with his son King Solomon, to whom this last psalm in a collection of David's prayers is addressed (see the opening and closing words). Inevitably, living up to such a calling in practice proved a challenge, as the kings we meet in 1 and 2 Kings demonstrate. Christians have understood this vision of the ideal king and kingdom to be fulfilled ultimately in Jesus and expressed through his church.

The psalm begins with its one clear request: to rule wisely and well in this way, expressing God's justice and righteousness, a human ruler needs more than their own resources. They need God's guidance in decision-making; God's goodness shaping the heart and mind.

God's concern is for Israel, but also for the nations (vv. 8–11, 17, 19). Their rulers will admire and acknowledge Israel's king, whose domain will spread widely – so that more of the poor and needy will be rescued from oppression through his rule (vv. 12–14).

As with Book 1, we find Book 2 of the Psalter rounded off with a coda, a brief doxology urging that praise be given to Yhwh, the God of Israel (vv. 18–19). Yhwh, who alone does wonders, is also Elohim, *the* God, who should be honoured by the whole earth.

Guidelines

- Did one of these psalms particularly catch your attention? Explore the reasons why. Is there a phrase or idea which stands out for you?
- We've noticed the number of laments in the first two books of the Psalter. How does this compare to the prayers and songs shared in your own church? Are you finding suitable ways to include lament in your worship? What kind of issues does this throw up for corporate worship?
- We've noticed links with other psalms (Psalm 57) and with the New Testament (Psalm 69). This might remind us how valuable and enriching it is to become more familiar with scripture as a whole, not just our favourite parts – and to reflect on how the different parts shed light on each other.
- Book 2 of the Psalter highlights God's commitment not just to Israel, but to all peoples and nations (Psalms 57, 65—67, 72). Let that emphasis on the wider world enlarge your horizons afresh. Where does it lead you – in your praying, reading, giving, campaigning, going?
- In Psalms 42—43 and 63, *nephesh* is sometimes translated 'soul'; yet it refers to a person's embodied life. Do you know people in your church or community who think we have disembodied souls, which go after death to a disembodied heaven? Does that way of thinking need challenging and deepening?
- In what ways can Psalm 71 help us all develop a positive attitude to growing older and facing the future? Which verse or idea in it do you want to embrace and perhaps share with others?
- In Psalm 72 we found a vision of leaders using power to serve the powerless – choosing compassion and justice, not coercion or self-enrichment. Think and pray into that inspiring challenge, as it speaks to politicians and heads of state – and also to the rest of us, as we exercise power in our different situations.

FURTHER READING

Sue Gillingham, *The Poems and Psalms of the Hebrew Bible* (Oxford University Press, 1994).

O. Palmer Robertson, *The Flow of the Psalms: Discovering their structure and theology* (P&R Publishing, 2015).

Malcolm Guite, *David's Crown* (2021).

Proverbs 1–9: an introduction to 'wisdom technology'

Peter Hatton

We think we're so clever. What we know (the items of information theoretically available to humanity) used to double slowly, perhaps every hundred years or so. Now the pace of information acquisition has accelerated so much that, some say, the amount we know doubles every year; and we seem to be doing more and more with this gigantic harvest of information. Hidden on our devices and on the internet, complex algorithms analyse our choices, our interests and our behaviour online, and target us accordingly with advertisements and suggestions for purchases, further viewing and consumption.

How strange then that, although we (apparently) know more than any previous generation, we continue to grapple with so many seemingly intractable issues, some of which appear to threaten the survival of our species. 'Informed' as we are, what explains our failure to tackle climate change, global poverty or wars? Moreover, paradoxically, we are repeatedly blindsided by 'black swan' events, unpredictable world-changing developments that, with all our IT, we fail to foresee – for instance, the near collapse of the financial markets in 2008, the coronavirus pandemic and the outbreak of a horrendous war in Europe.

The wisdom literature of the Old Testament never forgets that the world we live in is unpredictable and dangerous. Its aim, under God, is to help humanity navigate the treacherous waters of life. These books are informed by the experience of the sages who have gone before us and they also urge on us 'the fear of the Lord'; that is, a respect for, and a confidence in, a God who is ready and willing to help us face a future we can never wholly foretell.

Despite the opinion that Proverbs seeks to do this by putting forward a complacent, self-satisfied morality, this is a complex text which aims to get us to think, rather than simply accept what we have been taught. The first nine chapters prepare us for the rich, piquant feast of sayings that predominate in the last 22. They also have much to teach us as we seek to flourish in this beautiful but troubled world and to serve the God who is renewing all things in Christ.

Unless otherwise stated, Bible quotations are the author's own translation.

1 A risky endorsement

Proverbs 1:1

Proverbs' first word, *mishlē*, is a plural form of the Hebrew word *māshāl*, which is usually rendered 'proverb' or 'saying'. However, its literal meaning is 'to compare' or 'to rule'. So on the one hand, many of the book's sayings involve comparisons and contrasts (e.g. between the wise and the foolish, the wicked and the righteous); on the other, these sayings are empowering. They help us get a grip on our often-confusing reality.

The next words in the book's title point us to one in whom the two meanings of this root come together. Solomon was a *mōshēl*, a 'ruler'; indeed, Israel's most splendid king. He also 'spoke three thousand proverbs' (*māshāl*, 1 Kings 4:32). This reference does not mean that Solomon himself composed, or even collected, all the sayings in Proverbs. Given that some of the book's collections are ascribed to others (e.g. 'the wise' in 22:17; Agur in 30:1), that cannot be the case. Nevertheless, that Proverbs is a 'solomonic' book is deeply significant.

Solomon was remembered not only as a great, wise king of Israel but also as one who had friendly contacts with foreigners. He allied with Hiram, ruler of the powerful city of Tyre, who sent skilled craftsmen and materials to help build the temple in Jerusalem (1 Kings 5:1–12). The queen of distant, fabulously wealthy Sheba was drawn to hear his wisdom (1 Kings 10:1–13). By invoking Solomon at the beginning, Proverbs signals that the book's wisdom is not just narrow tribal lore; it is open to dialogue with others. However, the story of Solomon also flags up the risks in such dialogue. Prompted by foreign wives, he introduced idolatrous worship into Israel (1 Kings 11:1–8). Yet, somehow, he remains an acceptable patron for a complex enterprise which seeks to engage us beyond our comfort zone.

Read 1 Kings 10 and 11. We struggle with the paradox of a wise king who could be foolish. Yet we may also remember times when we heard wise words from those whose culture, even whose language, was foreign to us.

2 Education, education, education

Proverbs is one of only a few biblical books (Luke is another) that tells the reader what it intends to achieve. Verses 2–6 are a single long sentence in the Hebrew, although one divided into a series of clauses each using a grammatical form expressing strong intentionality. So verse 2 might be rendered (somewhat literally) as: 'In order that [you might] know wisdom and instruction; in order that [you might] understand perceptive words.' This chain of clauses asserts the book's purpose in the same vein to the end of verse 6.

Although most of the words used here (however translated) involve an increase of intellectual understanding, the expressions that round off verse 3 – 'justice and equity and right dealing' – confirm that a moral education is also intended. Furthermore, we are informed that Proverbs is aimed at more than one sort of reader. Yes, 'the naive' and 'the young' mentioned in verse 4 can benefit from its wisdom; but those who are already somewhat wise and perceptive (v. 5) can also build on their existing insights. Those who dismiss this text as simplistic are making a grave mistake, an insight which is reinforced by the talk in verse 6 of the 'riddles' and 'puzzles' of the wise.

We land in a claim that 'the beginning of knowledge is the fear of the Lord' (v. 7). The conventional English rendering here disguises the fact that the being to be 'feared' – that is, always respected; always remembered with awe and reverence in all our dealings – has a name, YHWH (often vocalised as Yahweh), the Holy One of Israel. Wisdom is to be found in relationship with this named God, whose love and whom the fear of are commended repeatedly in many other biblical books, not least Deuteronomy. Some commentators, bearing in mind that the phrase 'fear of YHWH' appears 14 times in Proverbs, have spoken of it as the book's 'logo', but this reference to slick modern marketing is misleading. Rather, such fear is the central, key value of Proverbs, an intentional attitude that must underpin our quest for knowledge and wisdom.

Look at other verses that mention 'fear of YHWH' in Proverbs 1:29, 2:5, 8:13 and 9:10. Do they help us understand what this key phrase means?

3 Home-schooling?

Who should be primarily responsible for the education of a child? While it cannot always be the case, surely this privilege and duty belongs naturally to the parents.

This, at any rate, is the assumption in these verses which – in line with the conventions of ancient instructional texts – assume a reader who is a young man. So his father has a crucial role to play, but so does, in a departure from other instructional texts in the surrounding cultures, his mother. The vocabulary used underlines the high seriousness of their joint endeavours: the father's 'instruction' (v. 8) is *mūsar*, which elsewhere is rendered 'discipline'. Moreover, the mother's 'teaching' is nothing less than *tōrah*, the word linked to the holiest of Israel's texts. No surprise, then, that these parental instructions are, as it were, precious adornments (v. 9), just as Deuteronomy 6:8 commands that YHWH's statutes are to be worn on the body.

We learn best, then, in relationship with others. However, Proverbs is very aware that, in contrast to the loving nurture of parents, there can be corrupt relationships in which bad things – selfishness, greed, violence – are passed on. Verses 10–19 warn against the gang mentality in which criminality is accepted as the norm and character is malformed with a bent towards wickedness. The end of this common enterprise is death.

Now comes something unexpected! It seems that humans are not the only, or perhaps not even the main, educators. The figure of Wisdom is active even in the business of human life, continually appealing to the simple for a hearing. Who is this woman? Her special, extraordinary nature is flagged up when she is called *hokhmōt* (v. 20). This is the plural form of the word for wisdom, literally 'Wisdoms'; a plural of majesty then, like the word 'Elohim' for 'God'. Yet this exalted woman yearns to be in relationship with us, simple and foolish as we often are, and grieves when we will not listen to her.

Can you remember a parent, teacher, pastor or friend who filled you with a passion to learn? Give thanks to God for their friendship and enthusiasm.

4 The call of the wild

A parental voice sounds again at the start of this chapter, urging the young learner to begin a search for wisdom and pointing them to the gracious desire of YHWH to lavish understanding on those who approach him in the right spirit of humility, respect and awe – that is, in 'fear' (vv. 1–8). Any who are prepared to seek this divine wisdom will be saved from those who seek to lead them astray (vv. 9–15).

Proverbs pulls no punches here in identifying and condemning the corrupt men who, perversely delighting in wickedness (v. 14), use all sorts of lies and deceit to mislead the unwary. Moreover, a malign female counterpart to *hokhmōt* 'Lady Wisdom', our reliable guide to life and happiness, is introduced to us in verse 16. This is the *îshah zārāh* ('strange woman'), the *nokhriyāh* ('foreign woman'). Translators often tone down the strangeness and foreignness of this dangerous character and translate 'adulterous woman' (or something similar) here. This doubtless comes from an understandable desire not to give any support for xenophobic attitudes to foreigners or to reinforce negative stereotypes towards women. However, it risks missing an important point.

The *nokhriyāh* is not meant to be a realistic portrait of a human being any more than her benign counterpart *hokhmōt* is a flesh-and-blood woman. Rather, she stands for the way in which, often enough, what is 'exotic' and 'other' has a powerful allure for us, while what is familiar seems mundane, even boring. It is not just in relationships that the grass is always greener on the other side! We live in a culture where, for instance, the supposed wisdom of eastern religious traditions (often very imperfectly understood) is held to be more interesting, more 'spiritual', than Christian teachings, and the extraordinary riches of Christian spirituality are neglected.

Do we not often crave novelty, the excitement of what seems strange and unknown, while neglecting what is routine and familiar? 'The trivial round, the common task, should furnish all we ought to ask' (John Keble, 1792–1866). Does it?

5 More precious than rubies

Again, we hear the voice of instruction from a parent to their child. At first sight, this teaching seems too good to be true. It appears that all things will go well for the devout God-fearer (vv. 7, 9–10) and seeker after wisdom (vv. 4, 13). We may recall the use made of these verses and others in scripture (e.g. Psalm 1) by those who teach so-called 'prosperity theology'. However, this teaching, that God will bless with material prosperity those who devote themselves sincerely to him, not only makes a mockery of the sufferings of the martyrs (and of Jesus himself) but it also only works by dragging selected verses out of context to serve the predetermined end.

We note first of all the passage's stern warning against all claims to wisdom rooted solely in human experience and desires and which leave God out of the picture. This mindset is what it calls 'leaning on our own understanding' (v. 5) and being 'wise in our own eyes' (v. 7). When we are so minded, we pursue our own goals without thought for their consequences for others and, perhaps, for ourselves. Considerable ingenuity and expertise can be deployed as long as we think we, or our group, will benefit; a gas chamber will be designed with the same careful diligence as an operating theatre.

In contrast, those who fear God will acquire the true wisdom that sees all things from the perspective of his kingdom and which leads to true prosperity. Genuine human flourishing, as verses 13–18 make clear, goes far beyond mere material prosperity measured by full storehouses and treasuries.

The mention of the 'tree of life' in verse 18 underlines this point. Not only is the tree of life a common image for true human fruitfulness throughout the ancient Near East but it is also, of course, the tree that flourished in Eden. There it sustained Adam and Eve before barns and treasuries were relevant or money and jewellery even thought of!

Do we live as if 'life were more than food and the body more than clothing'? (Luke 12:23)

6 With the grain of the cosmos

Proverbs 3:19–35

The bulk of this passage doubles down on the claim that the good things that flow from a life based on wisdom are not just material. They include that serene trust in God which gives us peace of mind even as we live in a world where material prosperity and health can be swept away in a moment (vv. 21–26). The good, wise life it portrays is one in which costly generosity is practised (vv. 27–28) and the ways of violence and oppression are rejected (vv. 29–31). It is also one lived in a confidence that God will see to it that, in the end, righteousness and virtue will triumph over sin and wickedness; that, as Martin Luther King, Jr, puts it, 'the arc of the moral universe is long but it bends towards justice' (vv. 32–35).

Is this just wishful thinking? Surely much experience points away from what appears to be a cosy but unrealistic picture. However, the passage grounds its optimistic vision in a profound claim about the nature of the universe we live in. It asserts that wisdom and understanding are built into the very fabric of our cosmos (vv. 19–20). Yes, seemingly chaotic, apparently random events may happen, but they are held within a broader framework that is rational and indeed intelligible.

It follows that true knowledge about the universe is possible; that, for instance, the astonishing enquiry into reality, based on reliable observation and driven by curiosity and wonder, which we call science, can lead to profound, true insights. Indeed, there are laws (e.g. those of thermodynamics) that can be established by investigation and can reliably predict what will happen throughout the cosmos.

Proverbs asserts that a wise, good life is lived in tune with this God-given rationality built into the universe. Folly and sin are signs that we are not in harmony with its foundational realities.

For reflection: 'The most incomprehensible thing about the universe is that it is comprehensible' (attributed to Albert Einstein).

Guidelines

For the past eight years I have included a class on Proverbs in the biblical theology module offered at the Bristol theological colleges. It is at master's level, so many of the students have already completed degrees in biblical studies elsewhere. At the beginning of the class I ask such students if as undergraduates they were taught (usually in an 'Introduction to the Bible' module delivered by someone who was not a specialist in the wisdom books): that Proverbs teaches a simplistic wisdom; that Proverbs asserts, without qualification, that the diligent and devout will always prosper while the feckless, lazy and faithless will come to ruin; and that Job and Ecclesiastes offer a more radical wisdom which questions the 'complacency' of Proverbs. I am no longer surprised, but remain shocked, that the students invariably nod their heads sagely and agree that that was, indeed, the understanding of these books they were taught.

This is a classic example of how a misleading consensus view can be passed on unchallenged, a phenomenon which is not, I'm afraid, confined to academia. We may grant that there are verses and passages in Proverbs which, taken out of context and without taking into account vital nuances and qualifications, seem to support such a reading of the book. However, the first chapters of Proverbs introduce us to a wisdom which is far from complacent. Indeed, while there is no doubt in these pages that being wise does lead to good things, these are never seen in purely material terms.

Moreover, attaining wisdom is not a matter of simply soaking up the insights of the ancients. There are numerous false trails that appear more exciting, more immediately rewarding, than the seemingly dull business of listening carefully to what those who truly love us offer us on this journey. This careful discernment is complicated by the fact that the search for truth and wisdom is along a contested path. Folly is loud and can be persuasive.

- What leads us to think that something is true and wise?
- Who, among those we know and love, have we found to be a reliable guide along the way?
- Can we recall times when we have been utterly convinced of something that now seems false or unlikely?

1 Marrying well

Proverbs 4

The voice that speaks in this chapter is once again that of a teaching parent, a father, addressing a son. However, the teacher was once a pupil himself. The instruction he now offers came originally from his father. Is this still relevant for us in a much less structured society, where patriarchal (and matriarchal) authority is much diminished in comparison with ancient Israel? Well, as a grandfather myself, I note that, even today, families have traditions. Wisdom, and folly, are still passed down through the generations.

Be that as it may, the content of the grandparental advice here involves one of the central concerns of the heads of ancient families (and perhaps even, secretly, of adults in modern families); namely, that the younger generation find life partners who will help them flourish. Here Wisdom is the 'bride' that the young man is commanded to 'get' (qenēh) by his elders (vv. 5–9). The imperative qenēh, appearing four times in these verses, normally means simply 'acquire' or 'buy'. Here, however, something far deeper is intended. Our most passionate emotions must be engaged in intentionally forming a lifelong relationship with Wisdom, whose presence in our lives will bring us honour (vv. 8–9) and length of days (v. 10). Even more importantly, with such a spouse at our side we will be kept from turning aside from the 'straight path' (v. 11; compare Matthew 7:14) and from walking in the evil paths of the wicked (vv. 14–19).

The language here is strikingly erotic and this physicality is emphasised again in the concluding verses (vv. 20–27) with their repeated references to parts of the body. Proverbs, and indeed the Bible in general, never sees us as disembodied intellectual beings. If we think that the pursuit of knowledge is a disinterested academic enquiry, we are already on the wrong path. Rather, we should yearn for wisdom and understanding, for truth and righteousness, as a lonely person yearns for a lover to whom they can open their heart and their whole being.

Are there causes that engage our passions? If not, why not?

2 Scam alert

This passage is dominated by the sinister female figure we have already met, the 'foreign', 'strange' woman, the 'outsider'. She offers the young man illicit pleasures that would take him away from the right path of faithfulness. Should he yield to her seduction, he will set himself up for a lifetime of regret, losing his wealth and strength and, even more precious, his good name (vv. 9–14). His father urges him to prevent this harsh fate by remaining 'intoxicated' (the Hebrew suggests someone staggering under the influence of strong drink) with the 'wife of his youth' (v. 18). Sexual double entendre abounds in the passage ('wells', 'springs of water'); the erotic surfaces undisguised in verses 19–20.

In a post-#MeToo era, this portrait of a female sexual predator is not, perhaps, very appealing. In extenuation, we might reflect that, since most ancient instructional material was conventionally addressed to a young man, the rather negative (to our eyes) gender dynamics here were unavoidable. We might transpose the roles and imagine a young woman being groomed and seduced by a powerful older man. We should also note the confidence that if the dangers of such situations are recognised, then they can be successfully resisted; 'forewarned is forearmed'!

Even as we acknowledge these difficulties, we should not allow ourselves to be distracted from the insights offered here, especially the seductive power that 'honied lips' and 'smooth words' (v. 3) have over all of us, male and female. How can we guard against words skilfully employed to mislead us to our destruction? The command to 'listen' with attention and discernment is repeated again and again in these chapters; it begins today's passage. Careful listening of this sort is a critical exercise. It asks such questions as: 'Is this person speaking trustworthy?'; 'Whose interests do they have at heart?'; 'Are they informing and even challenging me or just pandering to my desires?'

Can we recall occasions when flattering, plausible words misled us? How can we guard against such deception in future?

3 Risk addiction

A chain of diverse topics involving behaviours that the young must avoid now follows. It begins with a stern warning against guaranteeing the debts of another (vv. 1–5), which seems something of a digression from what has gone before. The striking commendation of the ant as a wonderful example of industry and a reproach to the lazy (vv. 6–11) also introduces something new. Admittedly, praise of hard work will prove one of Proverbs' core values (compare 10:4; 12:24; 20:13; 24:30–34). However, while the next section (vv. 12–19) contains a novel form – the numerical saying (vv. 16–19) listing the divinely condemned characteristics of a disruptive troublemaker – its target can be recognised as a variant on the wicked characters we have already met beforehand (e.g. 4:14–17).

Does anything link what seems to be a random grouping? Well, all of them involve great risks for very little return. Guaranteeing another's debts allows your fate to be determined by others. Choosing to do nothing when you could act leaves you at the mercy of events. Gossiping and stirring up trouble makes you enemies for little or no benefit to yourself. This impression is confirmed when the passage ends with another ringing condemnation of adultery. Stealing bread when you're hungry is dangerous, but starvation has its own logic (vv. 30–31); risking disgrace and the vengeance of an enraged husband for the pleasures of illicit sex is, by contrast, totally irrational (vv. 24–29, 32–35). The transgressive thrills of adultery stand here for the strange pleasure of doing things we know are risky and offer little reward, but are unable to stop doing. Drug use leads to addiction, but so do many other things.

There is a remedy. It is found in those commandments that shed light in our darkness and guide us on to safer paths (6:20–24). Because we forget so soon, these healing, warning words are to be worn like amulets as constant reminders of the danger we are in through our own folly.

What helps us remember the dangers of the riskier habits we're addicted to?

4 'That hideous strength'

Verses 1–5 circle back on much that has gone before. The parental voice warns once more against the strange, foreign woman. There follows (vv. 6–23) a vivid but disturbing episode in which she seduces and destroys a foolish young man by offering him sexual pleasures. She is portrayed as a bold, independent character (vv. 11–13), clever (v. 10) and self-confident, who takes control of the situation and is able to shape both it and the young man to her will, reassuring him that their illicit pleasures will not come to light (vv. 12–20). She has mastered persuasive speech (v. 21), as she demonstrates in words that, even in translation, are richly suggestive and attractive (vv. 16–18).

Indeed, in another context, such a feisty, feminine character might be admirable. Proverbs closes with the praises of the 'courageous wife', who shares many of the same traits as the woman here; she is, for instance, bold and forthright, capable and independent (31:10–31). However, the two women are on very different paths. The 'courageous wife' seeks the good of others and fears YHWH. The *nokriyāh*, it is hinted, is an adherent of one of the evil cults of the ancient world that sacrificed children to the pagan gods (vv. 14, 22–23). On a more symbolic level, she represents those idolatrous practices that, elsewhere in scripture, are spoken of as 'adultery' (Jeremiah 3:9; Ezekiel 23:36–45).

However, the focus here on a manipulative woman may trouble modern readers. Is this an example of how Proverbs is a 'patriarchal text' that always sees women as 'the problem'? The many positive feminine characters in the book suggest otherwise. We should also note the powerlessness of the 'patriarchal voice' in the story, who can only observe (v. 6) the car crash developing in front of him. The father here cannot 'lay down the law'. All that is left to him is to warn and appeal.

Have we ever felt powerless as we have seen others making big mistakes? What have we said in such situations? What have we prayed?

5 Cosmic wisdom

This astonishing chapter gives us strong grounds for hope that evil, for all its power, will not triumph. As if provoked by the *nokriyāh*, Wisdom raises her voice in the most public of places (vv. 1–3). Indeed, her appeal is not just to Israel but to the whole of humanity (v. 4), from the weak and naive (v. 5) to the powerful (vv. 15–16). She proclaims that her straightforward, upright, even noble (v. 6) teaching, in which a relationship with YHWH is central (v. 13), is the way for individuals and communities to flourish. Indeed, her whole speech (vv. 1–21) amounts to a point-by-point refutation of what the *nokriyāh* offers.

Moreover, these powerful words are backed by an astonishing claim; namely that Wisdom played a key role in creation. In verses 22–31 we are offered an alternative, complementary version of the great accounts of how the world came to be in Genesis. These verses assert that all God's manifold works were grounded in Wisdom; and she is not conceived here as an abstract principle, or a set of laws, but as a being who rejoiced and danced as the cosmos became a place in which humanity could live (vv. 30–31).

Who is this Wisdom? Scholars have speculated that she might be a relic of polytheism, even a consort of YHWH. More convincingly to my mind, theologians have not hesitated to identify her with the Word of God, the second person of the Trinity. Whatever the value of such theorising, it should not distract us from the central insight here – that the cosmos is grounded in, and in-dwelt by, a resplendent, joyful Wisdom for whom we must yearn and in whom we can find life. Evil and folly are, in the big scheme of things, superficial. They can be overcome by those who listen to the one who calls out to us in the beauty and rationality of creation and is graciously present in every discovery and true insight (vv. 32–36).

What helps us be lifelong learners? At the end of today, and of every day, let us reflect, 'What new things have I learned?'

6 Truth and lies

The chapter opens in a way that seems in tune with the optimism of the immediately preceding passages. Wisdom's house in its first verses is a holy place – temples in the ancient world commonly had seven pillars and were places of feasting and celebration. Her 'path of understanding' (v. 6), then, is a way of joy and holiness. Surely the simple cannot but respond to the invitation of her maids (vv. 3–6)!

We might think so, but the next section offers us a realistic corrective. Some people will respond angrily to any challenge to the way they live (vv. 7–8). Indeed, how we respond to a justified rebuke, offered in love, is a sort of litmus test of whether we truly fear YHWH and are on Wisdom's path (vv. 9–11). Verse 12 is puzzling; perhaps it emphasises that we cannot evade personal responsibility for the state of our souls – 'If you are wise, then you can have the wisdom described above, but if you are selfish, then you are on your own.'

Indeed, surprisingly, the final word in these introductory chapters is spoken by a character called 'the Foolish Woman' (ēshet khesîlut). Given that she is offering the simple 'know nothings' (v. 16) the same pleasures, exciting because they are transgressive (v. 17), that the nokhriyāh offered earlier, she may be regarded as another avatar of Wisdom's great opponent. Allowing this misleading, dangerous voice to speak is a risky strategy, even if her words come with a warning (vv. 13, 18). However, it is more perilous to seek to silence those who offer us nothing but lies. Forbidden from speaking in the public square, they can lure the unwary by posing as those whose truths are being censored by the powerful. Proverbs is confident that falsehood will, in the end, be exposed as such when it is brought into open dialogue with Wisdom.

How do we respond when challenged about our lifestyles, prejudices and ways of thinking? How do we react to the expression of views we don't agree with, and may even think are demonstrably false?

Guidelines

The sayings in Proverbs 1—9 seem to flit from one topic to another. Some assert that if we are devout, honest and diligent we shall thrive, but others contend that in an unjust world no good deed goes unpunished (e.g. 13:23; 22:7). Indeed, some sayings offer conflicting advice (e.g. 26:4–5)! We might reflect that these very 'defects' suggest how accurately the sayings material of Proverbs reflects our lives. After all, experiences do not come to us neatly arranged by theme, but in a rather confusing variety; often enough, the honest and hard-working get on but, often enough, they don't. We are surrounded by conflicting opinions and need the 'wisdom of Solomon' to decide what is right.

We can see how Proverbs 1—9 prepare us both for reading the rest of the book and for seeking, in the perplexing reality of our world, 'whatever is true, whatever is honourable, whatever is just, whatever is pure, whatever is lovely, whatever is commendable' (Philippians 4:8). These chapters take it for granted that we can be easily misled in our search for flourishing. Lying but plausible voices, careless of our true welfare so their own ends are served, seek to pull the wool over our eyes. Yet these chapters are also convinced that we can see through the deceits and come to real knowledge of the truth.

This confidence is grounded in Proverbs' belief that Wisdom is more deeply rooted in the cosmos than folly. Indeed, the Wisdom these chapters celebrate is on a mission. Yes, humans must search for knowledge, but when they do so they will discover that their curiosity is matched by a divine response, indeed has been prompted by a divine initiative. Wisdom wants both to disclose herself to us and to enter into a relationship with us. We are led to a 'Wisdom Christology', to the one who is the way, the truth and the life (John 14:6) and who promises, 'You shall know the truth and the truth shall make you free' (John 8:32).

FURTHER READING

The Bible Project, Proverbs: **bibleproject.com/explore/video/proverbs**

David Hutchings and Tom McLeish, *Let There Be Science: Why God loves science and science needs God* (Lion Hudson, 2017).

Tremper Longman III, *How to Read Proverbs* (IVP, 2002).

Ernest Lucas, *Proverbs (The Two Horizons Old Testament Commentary)* (Eerdmans, 2015).

St Francis of Assisi

Richard Martin

St Francis (feast day 4 October) was born in Assisi in 1181/82 and died in 1226. His life of faith, humility and simplicity in those 44 years has inspired and fascinated people ever since.

Many Christians see Francis as an exemplar of authentic discipleship, not only those who take vows in the First, Second and Third Orders of the Society of St Francis, but also those who admire aspects of his story: his care for the marginalised; his embrace of poverty; his friendship with the natural world; his engagement with Islam; his unease with ecclesiastical structures; his irrepressible joy.

The current Pope is the first to be called Francis, choosing the name because he too wanted to care for the poor, rejecting luxury and greed in the church and in society.

People of other faiths often accept his saintliness. On 27 October 1986 Pope John Paul II welcomed delegates to an ecumenical and inter-faith World Day of Prayer, saying, 'I have chosen this town of Assisi as the place for our Day of Prayer for Peace because of the particular significance of the holy man venerated here – Saint Francis – known and revered by so many throughout the world as a symbol of peace, reconciliation and brotherhood.'

He inspires people who hold no faith, too. Whether it is his understanding that all creation is to be venerated, the prayer 'Make me a channel of your peace' (not written by Francis but seen to be authentic in expressing his values) or just the custom of having a Christmas crib (Francis pioneered this idea at Greccio in around 1220), Francis' legacy is pervasive.

This week, we will look at some of the key moments in Francis' life in the light of the Bible, because Francis' whole life was based on obedience to what he read there.

Unless otherwise stated, Bible quotations are taken from the NIV.

1 'Francis, rebuild my church'

John 2:18–22

Francis, although he founded a community, often retreated to pray in solitude. One of the first stirrings of his particular call came in the Church of San Damiano, which was pretty much a ruin. As he prayed alone, he gazed at the picture of Christ on the cross behind the altar and heard his voice, 'Francis, rebuild my church.'

In his childlike obedience, he set about doing just that. He raised money and repaired the walls, levelled the floor and reinstated the roof, working with his own hands.

But Francis was not, it turned out, called to be a one-man ecclesiastical bricks-and-mortar taskforce. Instead, the vocation that emerged for him was to rebuild the church on its evangelical foundations of the humility and poverty of Christ. Not just one structure in Italy, but the whole Church of Rome.

Jesus encountered similar misunderstanding from people in his day. He spoke of the destruction and rebuilding of the temple: 'Destroy this temple, and I will raise it again in three days' (v. 19). But they assumed he meant Herod's edifice. Rather, he was referring to spiritual reality: his own death and resurrection: 'The temple he had spoken of was his body' (v. 21).

Repairing and re-ordering church buildings is an honourable and necessary task. Architects, surveyors and craftspeople to this day skilfully maintain heritage and reimagine the use of space. Many of us are stewards of magnificent or historically important buildings.

Francis' story reminds us that such work must be kept in perspective.

2 Lady Poverty

Francis did not merely accept poverty, nor did he just take a vow to be poor. He embraced it, he was in love with it, he married it!

He saw poverty as *the* way, first for himself and, later, for any who chose to go with him, to fulfil the absolute abandonment, obedience and faith that following Christ involved. The passage we read today he interpreted in a literal, childlike, radical (many said foolish) way.

This led to differences of opinion within his fledgling Order, even while he was alive. Some brothers wanted to accept gifts and to pursue study. Francis was deeply suspicious of ownership. If you own a book, you'll want a bookcase, then a room to keep it in, he argued.

In his youth, he had given away valuable assets of his father's. When his father hauled Francis before the church authorities to demand them back, Francis took off all (yes, all!) his clothes and flung them at his father's feet, in effect saying, 'There! You can have everything, if our property means so much to you!' A strategically placed clergy robe quickly preserved propriety.

In his adulthood, he would beg his food, lived in loaned accommodation (if you can call it that; sometimes it was no more than a ruin of a cattle shed) and delighted in being rejected with missiles and insults.

I suppose you could interpret this as a refusal to take responsibility. Or as a refusal to engage with structural injustice. Or as a sign of insanity.

But consider the countercultural possibility that there is deep wisdom here. If it is true that 'we brought nothing into the world, and we can take nothing out of it' (1 Timothy 6:7), what does ownership actually mean? And if 'the earth is the Lord's, and everything in it' (Psalm 24:1), is there not something almost blasphemous about claiming that any part of the earth's surface 'belongs' to us or to our tribe/nation?

Francis offers us a way of discipleship that is an antidote to consumerism. Perhaps we dismiss it too easily because it touches a raw nerve?

3 The encounter with the leper

Mark 1:40-45

You know how it is. One person cannot stand the sight of blood. Another can't bear their feet being touched. Another recoils at the thought of eye surgery. Francis had such a phobia. His was an irrational but deeply felt revulsion of leprosy. It nauseated him.

One day he met a leper on the road. He rode past, quickly. But then Christ spoke to his heart and, being Francis, he obeyed. He turned round and rode to the leper. He dismounted. He hugged and kissed the leper – and realised, in a flash, that he had embraced Christ himself. This was the start of a lifetime's ministry. From then on, he and his friars regularly visited a colony of lepers, taking them food. Today, at Van Mon in the north of Vietnam, there is a leper colony located next to the Red River, a mandatory relocation place for about 600 people who have acquired leprosy, medically known as Hansen's disease. This place has become a key charitable effort of the Conventual Franciscan Order and The Franciscan Sisters of Mary.

This part of Francis' story is echoed in the stories of many others. It reminds us of Jesus' own encounters with leprosy, not least in our Mark 1 passage. It also reminds us that when Jesus told the parable of the sheep and the goats (Matthew 25:31–46), he did not mean that every person can minister to those who are hungry, thirsty, incomers, naked, ill or imprisoned. The body of Christ does all these things, but every member does not.

Foodbank volunteers, hospital chaplains and prison visitors are carefully recruited, trained, vetted and supervised. You and I cannot just walk in and help, even if we wanted to. But actually, most of the time I'm glad the rules prevent me from doing these things!

Today, take time to thank God for those whose ministry takes them to people you are glad to avoid. But beware! Francis' story reminds us that God has a curious sense of humour.

4 St Francis and the natural world

This psalm is a wonderful song of praise to God. How often have you looked up at the night sky and wanted to throw wide your arms in glory at the beauty of the creation and its creator? Here we have a very ancient address to that creation. It is reflected in the Benedicite of the 1662 Prayer Book ('O all ye works of the Lord, bless ye the Lord') and the Canticle of the Creatures, written by St Francis ('Be praised, my Lord, through sister moon and the stars').

As the poet Gerard Manley Hopkins wrote, 'The world is charged with the grandeur of God.' Christians everywhere rejoice that God is the creator, and they call upon the whole world (not just its peoples) to praise him.

Francis believed that the whole world points to the glory of God and reflects his love and power. The wind and the rain, the sun and the stars, the animals and birds, fish and reptiles – everything in the whole of creation reflects a generous God who is multifaceted, who is imaginative and who has a child-like love of creativity.

Maybe we can take ourselves out into nature for a walk or a swim and rejoice that this world is so amazing. The coronavirus restrictions made us realise that we had spent so much time indoors that we had missed much of what is taking place all around us. We rediscovered the local, the wonders in our back gardens and parks, our window boxes and houseplants. From the first bee of the year entering our garden to harvest some early nectar, to the defoliation of trees and bushes in preparation for winter, nature is busy and changing all the year round. Will we continue to notice?

One point to ponder is that while a star or a blade of grass is speechless, and insects only hum and pigs grunt, they all rejoice in their creator. But how? How do clouds praise God, or how does the sun worship God? Perhaps this is where we need the ear of faith.

Can you, like Francis, feel the presence of God within the world? It is a humbling thing to behold – and it radically affects the way we treat it.

5 The encounter with the Sultan

If you ask people about St Francis, many will soon quote, 'Lord, make me an instrument of your peace.'

I said in the introduction to this week's notes that Francis almost certainly didn't write that, but it is authentic in the way that it expresses his values. The story of his visit to the Crusades and then to the Sultan explains why.

Francis believed that it was *not* God's will for Christians to fight the Crusades. In so believing, he contradicted the teaching of the popes of the time, who taught that it was the will of God. Francis felt sorry for the soldiers who were caught up by this erroneous teaching, and he made three attempts to go to Egypt to offer an alternative message.

On the third occasion, during the Fifth Crusade, Francis reached the army and tried to persuade the Christian troops to stop fighting, warning that they would fail in their aims. He taught that we should love especially those who we see as our enemies, 'because they give us eternal life'. The troops, predictably enough, ignored him. Their officers abused him.

In September 1219, he took a great risk and went across the battle lines and ended up being admitted into the tent of Sultan Malik al-Damil in Damietta, Egypt, initially on suspicion of being a spy. He did not argue or dispute with the Sultan, but freely acknowledging that he was a Christian, was allowed to share his truth. In return, he listened respectfully to the explanation of Islam given by the Sultan. The medieval stories of a trial by fire to 'prove' who was right are almost certainly imperialistic fabrications.

He stayed there perhaps three weeks as a guest, was given protection and was then sent away with a gift, a horn used in the Islamic call to prayer (you can see this horn in Assisi).

It is thought that the canticle he wrote when he got back to Assisi, 'The Praises of God', may have been his attempt to compose a Christian version of the 99 beautiful names of Allah that he heard while with the Sultan. Psalm 145 is perhaps the nearest we get to it in our Bibles.

6 The stigmata

Philippians 3:7–11

On day 1 we saw how Francis' call was first revealed to him as he gazed at the cross in the ruined chapel of St Damiano.

A few years later, a Franciscan monk, Jacopone da Todi (d. 1306), was diligently fulfilling his vows in a life of devotion to Christ crucified. But he was troubled, sensing God had more to ask of him. Eventually, and not without resistance, he realised what it was. It was not enough to venerate the cross or even to worship Jesus upon it. What he had to do now was to be willing to experience the cross himself.

The apostle Paul knew about this step on the Christian road: 'I want to know Christ – yes, to know the power of his resurrection and participation in his sufferings, becoming like him in his death, and so, somehow, attaining to the resurrection from the dead' (v. 10). It is the narrow gate that leads to eternal life.

St Francis, as he lay sick on Mount Verna in 1224, also experienced the cross in a unique way. Unless we dismiss as pure hagiography the eyewitness account of Elias, who after Francis died in 1226 saw his body, it seems plain that Francis received the five wounds of Christ, known as the stigmata. He tried to keep them secret, hiding his hands, feet and side under his clothing, but the monks who tended him began to notice scars and bloodstains and were sworn to secrecy. He did not want to become a spiritual celebrity or a focus of devotion. Instead, he understood that this was very personal: the beginning of the end of his mortal life – an end that came slowly, through two years of blindness, weakness, cold and loss of independence, yet filled with praise.

Perhaps some reading this are also somewhere on that final journey. You will probably not experience the stigmata, but the experiences of being pierced by needles and maybe drips will be familiar. Can you see them as 'participation in [Christ's] sufferings'? If so, how does that affect the way you respond to them and to those who administer them?

Guidelines

St Francis would not want us to end this week focusing on him, but on his Lord. Here are some Franciscan prayers that I have found helpful and commend to you:

We adore you, most holy Lord Jesus Christ, here and in all your churches throughout the world, because by your holy cross you have redeemed the world.

May the power of your love, O Lord, fiery and sweet as honey, wean our hearts from all that is under heaven, that we may die for love of your love, you who were so good as to die for love of our love.

My brother fire, outdoing all created things in splendour, the Most High created you mighty, fair and useful. Be kind to me at this hour, be courteous, for long have I loved you in the Lord. I pray the great Lord who created you to temper your heat now so that, burning me gently, I may be able to bear it.

O Father of the forsaken and Lover of the unloved, make us bearers of your presence to all. Teach us to walk in the poverty of your Son and to be among all people as those who serve; in the name of him who for our sakes became poor, Jesus Christ our Lord.

God our Father, you always delight to reveal yourself to the childlike and lowly of heart; grant that following the example of the blessed Francis, we may count the wisdom of this world as foolishness and know only Jesus Christ and him crucified, who is alive and reigns with you, in the unity of the Holy Spirit, one God, now and forever.

FURTHER READING

Brother Bernard, *Open to God: The Franciscan life* (Fount, 1986).

Murray Bodo, *Francis: The journey and the dream* (Orbis, 1988).

John Moorman, *Saint Francis of Assisi* (SPCK, 1982).

Richard Rohr, *Eager to Love* (Hodder, 2014).

Jon M. Sweeney, *When Saint Francis Saved the Church: How a converted medieval troubadour created a spiritual vision for the ages* (Ave Maria Press, 2015).

A bioethical toolkit

Ruth Bancewicz et al.

All of us have an important contribution to make to the body of Christ at every point in our lives, whether receiving or giving care or (more often) somewhere in between. Society does not always recognise this, and we can experience intense pressures to label or treat certain kinds of people as having more value than others. Throughout our journey we may also face difficult medical decisions, both for ourselves and for those we love, as well as the members of our churches.

We naturally turn to the Bible for encouragement that each person is of enormous value in God's eyes. We also look to scripture for answers to ethical decisions. When it comes to the big questions of modern medical ethics, however, the Bible has few detailed answers. Instead, we can find wisdom in its pages that we can apply in new situations.

This series looks at some of the most important questions and issues relating to the value of each person as an individual made in the image of God. Six writers share their insights on biblical passages that relate to issues around the beginning and end of life and care for the vulnerable. Our hope is that they will help you to grow in your understanding of Christian bioethics and to identify biblical principles that can be applied in the opportunities and challenges that you face in the coming years.

Unless otherwise stated, Bible quotations are taken from the NRSV.

1 The image of God

Rodney Holder

Genesis 1:26–27

What it means for humans to be made in the image (*ṣelem*) and likeness (*děmt*) of God has been debated in Christian theology down the ages. Irenaeus distinguished between these terms, 'image' denoting our rational nature and 'likeness' our moral virtue. He believed that at the fall humans retained the image but lost the likeness. In contrast, both Luther and Calvin recognised typical Hebrew parallelism here, so that no such distinction should be drawn.

Swiss theologian Emil Brunner took a view similar to Irenaeus. However, his colleague Karl Barth recognised the danger which Brunner's interpretation could lead to: those such as newborn children and adults who are not capable of exercising rationality or moral virtue could be rejected – a critically important matter during the Nazi period when the Barth–Brunner debate took place. Certainly the rational interpretation needs some qualification. At the same time, it offers an explanation of the remarkable consonance between the human mind and the cosmos, the fact that we can do science and understand the laws that shape the universe, from the smallest subatomic particle to the furthest galaxy.

Barth's own interpretation of the *imago* is fundamentally relational and widely accepted today: 'He sets man in fellowship with Himself as a being existing in free differentiation and relationship' (*Church Dogmatics*, III.1, 185). It is this capacity for fellowship with God, and with other humans, that marks us as unique among God's creatures and distinguishes us from the animals.

Our passage says that God has given humans 'dominion' over all other living creatures on the earth, and this provides another interpretation of the *imago*. Here the Hebrew verb *rādā* means 'to rule' or, indeed, 'have dominion over'. It does not mean 'exploit', 'trash' or 'render uninhabitable'. Far from it. Bearing in mind the divine image that we bear, indicating the fellowship we enjoy with God and our human brothers and sisters, and that God's nature is 'love', we are to rule as God's vicegerents, in other words, to rule in his place and as he would rule.

2 Care for the vulnerable

Ruth Bancewicz

Deuteronomy 10:12–22

This passage highlights three classes of people who represent the socially vulnerable, powerless or marginalised. God's intention for the Israelites was that they should reflect his character of justice and mercy by taking care of these people in their midst. They were to live out the greatest commandments: to love both God and neighbour. One motivation for this behaviour was to come from deep within their own identity: the fact that God protected them and showed them justice when they were weak and powerless while in slavery in Egypt.

This ethic is the very opposite of what we are led to believe is the driving force behind the living world: the struggle against all others for survival. It's true that competition for limited resources is key for every organism, but cooperation is also an incredibly important and ignored factor. Every major evolutionary transition – from molecules to cells, simple cells to complex cells, single cells to multicellular organisms, individual organisms to pairs of parents, and pairs to communities – has been accompanied by a step-change in cooperation. At the very centre of your being, and of every living thing on the planet, are organic components working together to achieve greater ends than they could on their own.

Genuine altruism – the ability to make decisions that don't benefit (or indeed actively work against) oneself even in the broadest sense – seems to be a uniquely human trait. But the key importance of cooperation in the created order does resonate with the divine command to care for others. Creation reflects something of its maker.

A second motivation for justice and mercy given in this passage is less altruistic: 'for your own well-being' (v. 13). Today we know the benefits of behaving in altruistic ways: interacting with other people, helping others and working together can increase our own well-being, even to the extent of boosting the immune system and reducing stress levels.

The Israelites did not understand the world in a scientific way, but their God-given law underscored the link between the care for vulnerable and marginalised people and the well-being of the whole nation. As the biologist and philosopher Jeff Schloss has said, 'It looks like we're really built to flourish when we give and receive care for others.'

3 Care for the suffering

Murdo Macdonald

These encounters, in all the synoptic gospels, form part of a series of confrontations between Jesus and Jewish religious authorities. Having been accused of blasphemy (2:1–12) and of eating with sinners (2:13–17), as well as quizzed about his attitude to laws around fasting (2:18–22), Jesus twice contravenes strict rules around behaviour on the sabbath (2:23—3:6). Jesus is under pressure – plots to kill him are afoot (3:6).

The middle sections in this barrage revolve around various aspects of eating, bracketed by accounts of restoration to health. The gospels depict Jesus performing a number of healing miracles, with a wide variety of beneficiaries. Women and men of a range of ages: some on the fringes of society (the blind beggar, those with leprosy); others, as here, God-fearing, respectable sabbath synagogue-attenders.

Not being in possession of full health is something which most of us will experience. Often this is only a temporary situation: recovery may come courtesy of our body's innate ability to heal or fight disease. Sometimes we require external assistance – thank God for antibiotics, prosthetics and surgery!

Health and well-being for all is prioritised in most societies. However, there is huge disparity in the resources available to achieve this: in developed countries, an average of more than US$4,000 per person is spent on healthcare each year, compared to only US$30 in the Democratic Republic of Congo. Even within affluent societies, there is a challenge in achieving equitable access to treatments, with the richest often able to 'queue-jump'. The lack of effective vaccine-sharing in the recent Covid-19 pandemic, leading to an estimated one million excess deaths in developing countries, is surely shameful.

Sometimes the challenges are about more than simply resource allocation. Our ability to intervene at the very beginning of life – with for example assisted reproductive technologies or prenatal diagnostics – can be helpful, but also presents ethical dilemmas as to the contexts in which they should be used. At the end of life, palliative care is often the ignored 'Cinderella' specialty, while debates rage around inappropriate interventions to prolong life and assisted dying.

We give thanks for advances in medical technologies, but long to see all people everywhere being able to live to their full potential.

4 The unborn child

John Bryant

Psalm 139:13–16

From fertilisation to first breath – an amazing developmental journey from single cell to living infant. For the first few days, the tiny embryo is not yet attached to its mother. At around six days after fertilisation, the embryo implants into the wall of the uterus to establish a pregnancy and then starts to grow into a baby. (Note: in medical terminology, the embryo becomes a fetus early in pregnancy.) As a biologist, I understand a lot about this developmental process, but I continue to regard it – and the very precise way in which it is controlled – with awe. The psalmist can have known very little about how embryos/fetuses develop, but his poetic appreciation – 'I am fearfully and wonderfully made' (v. 14) – certainly hits the mark.

The pre-implantation embryo was completely unknown to biblical writers. However, this tiny ball of cells has become familiar to us because of IVF, in which the pre-implantation phase is equivalent in time to the passage of the early embryo down the Fallopian tube. But how are we to regard these early embryos? In law they do not have the status of human persons. Some Christians disagree with this, suggesting that even one-cell embryos should be treated as persons. This would have significant implications for the practice of IVF, including the routine creation of 'spare' embryos and genetic diagnosis in order to reject embryos with particular genetic conditions.

Consideration of the fetus developing in the womb leads on to thinking about the deliberate termination of pregnancy. It is a topic that has divided and continues to divide Christians. Further, it also challenges our basis for ethical decision-making because the Bible is completely silent on abortion, although Exodus 21:22–25 suggests that fetuses were not valued as highly as people who are already born.

Psalm 139:13–16 is often quoted in support of prohibiting abortion, but surely cannot be read that way. As the conservative theologian and ethicist Richard B. Hays says of this passage, 'It must be interpreted within the poetic genre to which it belongs, not as a scientific or propositional statement.' Our decisions will have to be made not on the basis of specific 'rules', but on general principles applied with wisdom and compassion. We note that throughout scripture, a child is regarded as a gift from God and also that there is a general presumption in favour of life.

5 Disability and gene editing

Keith Fox

2 Corinthians 12:6–10

Today's passage reflects on the apostle Paul's 'thorn in the flesh'. Many people think that this adversity refers to a bodily ailment, reminding us that there is more to life than physical perfection. God's will for our lives includes much more than good health and he can work for his glory in circumstances that we might not choose. We thank God that scientific advances over the past hundred years have had dramatic effects on human health, including antibiotics, anticancer agents and drugs for treating mental illness. Within the past ten years, scientists have even developed technologies for altering our genes (DNA), raising the possibility of curing genetic diseases. However, some people consider that this is a step too far, and that this is 'playing God'.

It is fraught with many ethical questions, but healing and restoration have always been part of Christian ministry. We should ponder Jesus' question, 'Is it lawful to do good or to do harm on the sabbath, to save life or to kill?' (Mark 3:4). We must not accept disease too readily with a misplaced fatalism that sees everything as God's will. There are many tragic genetic diseases that lead to early childhood death, for which arguments in favour of gene editing seem compelling. On the other hand, enthusiasm for gene editing can avoid questions of how society includes people with disabilities.

Paul's 'thorn in the flesh' reminds us that what seems like a disease and weakness may be a strength, and that God's 'power is made perfect in weakness' (v. 9). There is more to living a fulfilled life than physical ability. All people have worth and we are precious because of what we are – made in God's image – not because of what we can or cannot do.

A common misconception is that improvements in health justify any intervention. However, there are many people whose strength comes from what seems like disease and weakness. Are we in danger of reinforcing an 'ableist' mentality, which assumes that independence and health should be maximised at all cost? An overzealous acceptance of gene editing can avoid questions of how we respect the people who regard their disabilities as alternative and equally valid ways of living. We all need to learn from these people.

So thank God for scientific advances that are part of God's way of alleviating human suffering. However, pray that these will be used responsibly, and honour those for whom God's grace and power is demonstrated in weakness.

6 End of life

Andrew Perrett

Genesis 25:7–10

Abraham had lived 100 years beyond the time when God called him to set out from Harran at the age of 75. God's promises of descendants and land were being fulfilled, and God's personal promise to Abraham of a long life ending peacefully (Genesis 15:15) was now realised. The time had arrived for Abraham to breathe his last breath. Hidden in this phrase is a reminder not so much of the interruption brought by death as the fact that every breath is a gift from our life-giving God. In each breath we take, God shows himself faithful.

Abraham's death is described in terms of homecoming – he was gathered to his people. God's promises looked beyond Abraham's life on earth; it was Abraham's time to go home – not to Harran, but to his people, the people of God. His homecoming was both physical and spiritual. His sons buried him in the place where he had lived (Genesis 13:18), the land he had bought to bury his wife Sarah (Genesis 23:10–18) and where later generations would follow (Genesis 49:29–32).

Whether or not Abraham's final days were uncomfortable, we are not told. We are told he was at peace: death held no power over him to trouble or frighten him. Abraham had learned to trust God's faithfulness: he was not surprised or unready to go home. He neither threw his life away nor clung to it with desperation. He had known this moment would arrive, though perhaps not exactly when. He had made the necessary practical arrangements and told his family what was to be done.

Abraham appears to have died with contentment, prepared in heart and spirit. His was a life well lived, despite some low points of his own making along the way. He valued life as a gift but understood that this part of his journey must end. He died with the certainty of God's promises continuing beyond his earthly life. The lives of God's people are not given up in resignation to death but are given up in recognition of hope. Life is to be celebrated as a testimony to God's faithfulness in the past and anticipated with the joy in coming home to be with God, beyond the shadow of death under which we abide for now.

Guidelines

To absorb the material from the week more deeply, reflect or act on it, do one of the activities below.

- **Pick an issue**: Which of the topics discussed this week was the most pertinent for you – perhaps in a pastoral situation or in your own family? Prayerfully go back over the passage and notes and jot down a biblically focused response to the issue in your own words.

- **DIY bioethical toolkit**: What do you think are the most important biblical principles that could guide your own bioethical decisions in the coming years? Once you've made a list, go back through the week's readings and see if you missed out anything important. If you're short of inspiration or time, you could abandon DIY and skip to stage two, making a list of the principles provided.

- **Make a change**: Looking back at the week's notes, which issue challenged you the most in terms of your own beliefs or behaviour? Is there something you need to do, or a question you need to follow up, in response to it? Prioritise time in the coming week to do something about it.

- **Further reading**: Pick something from the list below and make time to read, listen or watch it in the next week or so.

FURTHER READING

Ruth Bancewicz, *Wonders of the Living World: Curiosity, awe, and the meaning of life* (Lion, 2021).

John Bryant and Linda la Velle, *Introduction to Bioethics*, second edition (Wiley, 2018). (Written by Christians for a secular audience.)

Alexander Massman and Keith Fox, *Modifying our Genes: Theology, science and playing 'God'* (SCM Press, 2021).

John Wyatt, *Dying Well* (IVP, 2018).

'Thinking About…': **cis.org.uk/resources/thinking**.

The Faraday Papers: **faraday.cam.ac.uk/resources/faraday-papers**.

Explore the bioethics section of the Faraday lecture library (audio/video): **faraday.cam.ac.uk/resources/multimedia-category/bioethics**.

The Church of Scotland Society Religion and Technology Project downloadable resources: **churchofscotland.org.uk/about-us/our-views/science-and-technology**.

Matthew 24—28

Andy Angel

As we move into the final part of Matthew's gospel, we come up against some of its most moving and powerful teaching. As Christian readers, we cannot read the story of the passion unmoved – that the Son of God gave his life that we might be set free from sin, the devil and death. I say, 'come up against', as we also find in this familiar story some surprises and things which are deeply countercultural – notably, the obedience of the Son to death on a cross which, in early Christian circles, soon became celebrated as an example to us all (Philippians 2:1–11). There are also teachings which are challenging because they cause us to question some of our assumptions as we work through them.

We begin these final studies on Matthew with a week looking at this last sort of challenge. Jesus' words, 'This generation will not pass away before all these things have taken place' (Matthew 24:34), cause us trouble because that generation has passed away and yet the end of the world has not yet come (which is what many of us have been taught Jesus was talking about prior to those words). Some try to change the meaning of 'generation' to stretch the time limit, but that does not work because Jesus also said, 'Some standing here will not taste death before they see the Son of Man coming in his kingdom' (Matthew 16:28).

Some think that Jesus was wrong. Others claim that Jesus was not talking about the second coming but about the destruction of the Jerusalem temple in AD70. But if this is the case, did Jesus ever teach that there would be a final judgement when justice will be restored to the world? Or if Jesus has already come, as some claim he has, then many of us are left asking, 'Was it worth the wait?', because justice has not been restored to the world and many things are still manifestly very wrong with life on this planet.

Matthew 24—25 raises difficult questions and working through them is not easy, but we will tackle them head-on this week and, I hope, discover how Jesus spoke of justice among God's people in that generation and a hope of justice for all generations to come.

Unless otherwise stated, Bible quotations are the author's own translation.

1 Judgement on Jerusalem

Matthew 24:1–35

Those who enjoy predicting the end of the world will often pick up 'signs' from this text (and its parallels in Mark and Luke) when suggesting that some political event means that Christ is coming soon. However, the truth is that every event listed happened in the first century AD. The apostle Paul would even have included preaching the gospel to the ends of the earth (v. 14; compare Romans 10:18). So, in tackling the difficult words of verse 34, I want us to start with some background understanding.

Since the tenth century BC, the covenant people described the mighty acts of God in terms of his appearance as a heavenly warrior and storm god (technically, the theophany of the divine warrior). This pictured God coming in thunderclouds, the earth reeling and the heavens turning dark at his presence, as God came to defeat his enemies (e.g. Psalm 18). Jesus' words in verses 29–31 quote three texts which use this ancient mythic image (Isaiah 13:10; 34:4; Daniel 7:13). In Isaiah, God comes to defeat the wicked cities of Babylon and Edom. In Daniel, the son of man comes to receive authority over the world rescued from the power of the beasts, which represented kingdoms oppressing the covenant people. Jesus seems to use this myth in very much the same way, only with a twist in the tail of his prophecy. His disciples ask when the Jerusalem temple will be destroyed (v. 3) and Jesus seems to answer them in verses 29–31. The Son of Man will come as the divine warrior to destroy a wicked city, but this time it is Jerusalem. So Jesus uses the mythic language of his culture (Second Temple Judaism) in the way his contemporaries used it, to describe the action of God defeating his enemies, except that Jesus now identifies those in the covenant people who will not repent precisely as God's enemies.

Reading Jesus as using this language in the way his contemporaries used it raises questions which we will begin to answer as the week goes on. But, for the moment, it would be wise to note the spiritual lesson of this prophecy for the covenant people down the ages: to continually examine ourselves, ask God's forgiveness and turn to follow him afresh.

2 One taken, one left

Jesus continues his prophecy of Jerusalem's destruction. Reading the Old Testament prophets helps in understanding this text. In the prophets, you notice that God promises action (salvation or judgement) and uses human agents to do this. In Isaiah 40—55, God promises to free the Judeans from exile in Babylon and he uses the Persian king Cyrus to do it (Isaiah 45:1). In Habakkuk, God promises judgement and he uses Babylon to do this (Habakkuk 1). Time and again God uses human agents to do his will. Even in texts like Psalm 18, where God comes in theophany to rescue the Davidic king, we find that God does this through empowering the king in battle. So we should not be surprised if Jesus uses the language of theophany in the same way. We know from the parallel text in Luke 21:20–24 that Jesus does precisely this, as those verses describe foreign armies besieging Jerusalem, just as the Roman army did in the years of the Jewish War, AD66–70.

This helps us to understand better a controversial feature of this text: the two in the field and the two grinding meal, one of whom will be taken and the other left (vv. 40–41). Contrary to some teaching in certain churches, the one who is left is the one who is blessed. The one who is taken is taken by the Roman army as it moves through the nation crushing the revolt. This is not about anyone being taken to heaven. Again, the parallel with Luke makes this even clearer when the disciples ask where they will be taken and Jesus responds, 'Where the corpse is, there the vultures [or eagles] will gather' (Luke 17:37, NRSV). Vultures gathering over a corpse is hardly a fitting description of the kingdom of heaven. However, eagles (a symbol of the Roman army) gathering around the dead fits Romans killing their enemies all too well.

Again, reading the text within its cultural context sharpens our sensitivity to the message. Jesus prophesies that his people should flee – and during the Jewish War many did flee to Pella and saved their lives as a result of their obedience to the word of their Lord. There is a message in that for us all.

3 Slave parable (1)

Forgive the slightly dull title for today's reflection, but I want to highlight how cleverly Matthew structures this final teaching discourse of the gospel. The discourse divides into five parts. The two outer parts (24:1–44 and 25:31–46) mirror each other, as they are both speeches about the coming of the Son of Man. The second and fourth parts (24:45–51 and 25:14–30) also mirror each other, as they are both parables about wise and lazy servants and share a punchline. The parable of the bridesmaids falls in the middle. Today we look at the first of the servant parables.

The parable begins with a question which relates back to Jesus' teaching on the coming of the Son of Man against Jerusalem. The question asks in the light of the coming judgement against the nation, who really is the faithful servant of God, to whom God can entrust his covenant promises? Jesus responds to his own question with a blessing. He blesses the slave whom the master finds doing their work dutifully when he arrives. In other words, God will bless those whom God finds doing the work which God has set them on the day the Son of Man comes. When that day comes, God will put those servants in charge of his covenant promises and people. But Jesus follows this blessing with a warning, that no slave decides to take advantage of the master's absence and behave badly. This seems to be a warning to members of the early Christian community not to take advantage of each other or to engage in unholy behaviour before the Son of Man comes.

I will explain further later in the week, but this parable does double service. It speaks to those first-century Christians who were waiting for the Son of Man to come against Jerusalem, as happened in AD70, encouraging them to remain holy. It speaks to us also, as we wait for Jesus to come again. Through this parable, Matthew encourages us to remain steadfast to the commitment we made in repentance (when we first chose to follow Christ): to turn away from sin and walk daily in the righteousness Jesus teaches us, living out his commands in loving and joyful obedience.

4 The bridesmaids

While many of us may have sung the old chorus 'Give me oil in my lamp, keep me burning', I wonder how many of us ever stopped to ask what on earth we were singing. What was the oil we were asking for and why did we want to burn until the break of day? This parable, together with one of Jesus' judgement sayings, takes us to the biblical material at the heart of that song and explains it. The clue lies in the similarity between this parable and Jesus' teaching in 7:21–23. Just as certain people say to Jesus, 'Lord, Lord,' in Matthew 7, so the foolish bridesmaids call the bridegroom 'Lord, Lord' (v. 11). Just as Jesus said to those people, 'I never knew you,' so the bridegroom says to the foolish bridesmaids, 'I do not know you' (v. 12). The parable echoes Jesus' earlier teaching.

According to 7:23, the reason Jesus will tell certain people that he never knew them (and so will not permit them to enter the kingdom of heaven) is because they are (literally) 'workers of lawlessness'. They may cast out demons, prophesy and do mighty works in his name, but they fail to live out his teachings. Bringing this back to the parable, it is pretty clear that the oil in the bridesmaids' lamps is their holy living – our holy living.

The parable ends up asking interesting questions of contemporary faith. We may be mixing with people who take the call to holiness seriously, but do we? Are we too reliant on the faith of others to see us through? How long do we think we can continue living like this? The parable gives a snappy answer to that latter question: not a moment longer, because you simply do not know when Jesus will come again and you are called to a life of holiness, not a life of relying on the holy people around you. So the old chorus has a good deal of life in it yet – encouraging us to cry out to God for more of his holiness in our lives, that in all we say, think and do, we might burn for him until light dawns and his kingdom comes on earth as in heaven.

5 Slave parable (2)

Matthew builds on the first slave parable here. The theme remains the same as the previous two parables: that judgement will come and the slaves ought to be ready for it. However, Matthew develops certain themes in this second slave parable and I would like us to focus on one of these: the master entrusts his own money to the slaves. (Incidentally, this is why the master has every moral right to criticise the third slave as he does, because the expectation was that the slaves would invest the money as the master would have done.) You cannot press every point in a parable as if it were an allegory, because not all Jesus' parables work like that. However, there does seem to be an interesting parallel between the entrusting of money and holiness in the Matthean Jesus' teaching.

We can sometimes feel harshness coming out of this parable: that the master is as mean as the third slave suggests. When we read it as the third parable in a row, we can feel this even more keenly, as we feel judged already. But just as the slave was entrusted with money, so we are entrusted with holiness. Jesus does not expect us to find holiness by ourselves. He expects to have to teach us and train us in holiness. He expects to have to be gentle, patient and focused on us as he teaches and trains us (see 11:28–30). So we do not need to be afraid of holiness. Nor should we see holiness as a goal we have to achieve under threats from an almighty bully, because *God himself* does the work in us. Rather, we need to be open to the transforming work of Jesus.

That final slave epitomises the mindset we are to avoid: seeing God as angry, unfair, demanding and unjust – and so avoiding our responsibility to accept God's gift of training in holiness and burying it away as if it did not exist. Instead, we are to open ourselves up to this gift and allow the Lord Jesus to train us and transform us as he sees fit.

6 Judgement on all nations

We come to the final section of this discourse, which again talks about the coming of the Son of Man. However, the audience is not the same. Those who see the Son of Man coming in 24:29–31 are, in Greek, *pasai hai phulai tēs gēs* ('all the tribes of the land'), words Matthew quotes from the Septuagint (Greek) of Zechariah 12:12–14, where they refer to the twelve tribes of Israel. So, the audience as the Son of Man comes in judgement on Jerusalem is the twelve tribes of Israel. Here in Matthew 25:31–32, the audience and those who will be judged are, in Greek, *panta ta ethne* ('all the nations'). So the audience is different. Matthew works like Paul: God judges the Jew first, and then the Greek/Gentile (Romans 2:9–11).

This makes this passage refer to what we call the Second Coming of Christ. (Interestingly, there is no time limit on it, unlike the judgement in Matthew 24:1–44.) Blood, sweat and tears are poured out preparing sermons on this passage, as so often people think of it as contradicting Paul by teaching salvation by works. But this is a misreading. The kinds of actions of which Jesus approves here flow from a life lived following Jesus as teacher, allowing him to transform our lives so that we live according to his teaching. Such lives are utterly grace-filled. Such lives only begin with repentance. Lives which start in repentance but never move on to growing in grace are grace-stunted (and Jesus has already spoken about those in the parable of the sower, 13:18–23). The chief mark of grace in such lives is found in their humility. They ask Jesus when they did these things (vv. 37–39), unlike the unrighteous who make a rather snappy reply almost accusing Jesus for accusing them (v. 44). We should not conclude that Matthew contradicts grace here (let alone that Jesus has a different gospel from Paul), as both Jesus and Matthew knew that grace does not stop with initial forgiveness. Jesus loves us so much that he accepts us as we are, and Jesus loves us too much to leave us as we are. True grace always transforms our lives.

Guidelines

The interpretation of the texts we have looked at this week can cause no small controversy. I hope not to have caused too much this week, although I realise that some of the things that I have mentioned might be new to some (and possibly old news to others). If there is anything I want to encourage you to consider, reading Matthew 24 and 25, it is that we can have confidence in our future hope and so act in the light of its reality. There are influential schools of thought within theology which claim that Jesus was wrong about his coming before his own generation passed away. However, these schools of thought base their ideas on poor (and historically outdated) understandings of the function of the language of the theophany of the divine warrior. At the time of Jesus, this language could be used to refer to God's judgement at the end of time, but it was also used to refer to God's acts of salvation and judgement within history. If anything, at the time of Jesus, this language was used more often to refer to God's actions within history than at the final judgement. Matthew has Jesus use the language in both ways. In 24:1–44, Jesus talks of judgement on Jerusalem – a judgement within history. In 25:31–46, Jesus talks of the judgement on the nations – the final judgement which leads into the creation of the new heavens and the new earth, and the eternal kingdom of God.

I want to encourage us all not only to have confidence in our future hope but also to have confidence in talking about it. We may need to overcome our own fears and apprehensions around that day. But we ought to have confidence that it will be a day of justice – indeed, the Day of Justice when, finally, all wrongs will be righted. This ought to be something to celebrate about our God. We ought also to have confidence that we do not face that day in our own strength (or avoiding the idea that God really will judge us) but as people whom the Lord Jesus Christ loves to serve through teaching us how to live each day of our lives.

1 'All these things'

Matthew 26:1–25

Matthew kicks off the passion narrative with this innocent-looking phrase, literally translated 'and it came to pass when Jesus finished all these words' (v. 1). It is actually a key marker in Matthew's story of Jesus. The phrase 'and it came to pass when Jesus finished' has occurred four times already in the gospel (7:28; 11:1; 13:53; 19:1). Each time, it begins the narrative after a major block of Jesus' teaching. Twice Matthew writes, 'And it came to pass when Jesus finished these words' (7:28; 19:1). Now Matthew writes '*all* these words'. That is, the words are now complete – Jesus has delivered his teaching.

This is an important moment in the gospel narrative. Jesus has come to teach the true and final interpretation of God's commandments (23:8). The disciples are to listen to Jesus and learn from him (11:28–30). The disciples are to listen only to Jesus' voice, as no other interpretation of God's commandments is to be trusted (23:1–10). The disciples are soon to be commissioned to teach the nations how to live according to all Jesus' commandments (28:19–20).

We far too easily slip into the passion narrative, thinking that this is what it is really all about – Jesus dying to save sinful humanity. That is surely absolutely central to our faith, but it is not the end of the matter. Really, it is very much the beginning. Grace starts at the cross, unfolds in our lives as we learn from the one true teacher how to live afresh and then launches us into eternity with our loving and merciful maker and redeemer. Matthew uses this innocent phrase to link the ministry of Jesus pouring his grace into our lives by teaching us how to live with the grace he pours into our lives from the cross. We are to live as a people who accept the fullness of his grace. We must not treat the gospels as passion narratives with extended introductions (borrowing Martin Kähler's phrase), or treat Jesus as someone who hung around training his wayward disciples before getting on with the real business of saving the world. Rather, we should enjoy the multifaceted nature of the grace that pours into our lives.

2 Something shockingly new and wonderful

Matthew 26:26–29

Jesus does something remarkable with the Passover celebration. He takes two elements of the meal (the bread and the wine) and imbues them with radical new meaning.

When Jesus told his disciples the bread was his body, this must have been shocking. They have taken some time not getting their heads around his passion predictions – even resisting them (e.g. 16:21–23). They come to the meal that celebrated more than any other the freedom God won for his people from their political oppressors, and Jesus imbues this celebration meal with overtones of his death.

That was nothing compared with his comment on the wine. Blood ratified and sealed the first covenant (Exodus 24:1–8). So Jesus claims that his blood will ratify and seal another. At their celebration of the wonderful covenant God made with Moses, Jesus predicts its successor. Using the language of 'pouring out' the blood, Jesus evokes the sacrificial system and compares his death with a sin offering as he claims his blood is poured out for the forgiveness of sins (v. 28). Having recently predicted the destruction of the Jerusalem temple and so of the place where sacrifices were offered for sin, Jesus now tells his disciples that his death is the place where sacrifice is offered for sin. Just as Jesus predicted that he would give his life as a 'ransom instead of many' (20:28), so now his death as a sacrifice for sin is on behalf of many.

Jesus takes two elements of the Passover and transforms them. They were symbols of liberation, of freedom from oppression and of entering the land of promise. Now they are symbols of his death. On the day they celebrated the political liberation of the nation, he predicted the death of the Messiah. But, in and through that death, God was at work bringing not just his people but many into a new covenant relationship, which will result in many entering the kingdom of God. Much as Jesus overturned one hope with news his disciples clearly could not bear, the truth of his words has resulted and will result in the dawning of an even better hope. When Jesus' words overturn our hopes and dreams, it is always best to listen and obey.

3 I will never desert you

There is a deeply ironic ring about the words of Peter, 'Though all become deserters because of you, I will never desert you'(v. 33). The passage we read today begins with Jesus' prophecy of his disciples' desertion as they move out to the Mount of Olives ('This very night you will all fall away on account of me', v. 31) and ends with their deserting him when Jesus was arrested ('Then all the disciples deserted him and fled', v. 56). To be fair to the disciples, Jesus had predicted his crucifixion and they would have been aware that people who were crucified were executed alongside their followers. Jesus was the only Jewish 'messiah' whose followers were not killed alongside him. Suspecting his arrest would lead to their crucifixion, you can understand why they fled.

But there is a deeper irony to these words – that it is Peter, not Jesus, who speaks those words. Jesus embodies these words in his actions. The disciples all desert Jesus, but he does not desert them. He has committed to giving his life 'as a ransom for many' (20:28). The moment for him to accomplish this has come. He prays three times for this cup to pass from him, but three times also prays that the will of his Father be done. When the crowd come to arrest him, Jesus knows he could call down a very large army of angels to strike them down, but he does not. He acts in the way that means that the Father's will is done. Jesus begins the process of literally giving his life away so that many might have life instead of him. This act of self-sacrifice is stark.

Yet this reveals who Jesus truly is to all of us. Jesus is the one who will truly never desert us. He will always remain faithful to the will of the Father. He is utterly faithful and trustworthy – despite our unfaithfulness and untrust-worthiness. What grace!

4 Blasphemy!

The irony continues in the court scene where the council tries Jesus. The high priest asks Jesus if he is 'the Messiah, the Son of God'. The phrase 'Son of God' meant many things in the Old Testament. A 'son' of God could be an angel, a particularly righteous person, the Davidic king or the coming Messiah. So when the high priest asks Jesus if he is the Messiah, he uses the phrase 'Son of God' to mean the Messiah. Jesus does something quite extraordinary in his reply. He identifies himself as the 'Son of Man' of Daniel 7:13, whom Matthew interprets as a divine figure (24:29–31). Jesus begins his reply with the words 'I am', alluding to the name by which God identifies himself in Exodus 3:14. So, in his reply, Jesus not only identifies himself as the Messiah but as God himself. Small wonder the high priest cries out, 'Blasphemy!'

Believing that Jesus is God, we might look at the response of the high priest and the council and regret their inability to see and believe – even when Jesus tells them who he is. But here there is an even deeper irony in the way in which Matthew tells the story of Jesus. The Jewish leaders might totally reject Jesus here and decide that he deserves death, but his disciples have already deserted him to death. Even Peter follows only 'from a distance' (v. 58). The ease with which the disciples have hoped for the replacement of the Jewish leaders by themselves as leaders of the nation (20:20–24) has already been replaced with the ease with which they desert and distance themselves from Jesus when the challenging times come.

All of this poses the question for us: where are we with the claims of Jesus? They are not always comfortable. Following Jesus' teaching can be truly countercultural and bring us into conflict (or profound disagreement and difference of lifestyle) with those around us. How do we respond? Are we like the Matthean disciples, who talk the talk and then run, rather than remaining firm when the time of testing comes? One day the Son of Man will come and the question we all need to ask is what will he find us doing.

5 Defining moments (1)

Peter is one of those characters in the gospels who captures the imagination and provokes comment. There are certain points in his life which people remember and somehow those moments define Peter in our understanding. Of all those events in his life, this must be the most likely to do so. Jesus has predicted that Peter will betray him. Peter has denied it. Now, just as Jesus said, before the cock has crowed three times, Peter has denied Jesus.

Those words 'and he went out and wept bitterly' (v. 75) are worth pondering a moment. Peter knows he has let Jesus down. He knows he has failed. He knows he has betrayed the person he was sworn to follow to the point of death. He has reneged on his commitment to Jesus. He has publicly declared that he is no longer signed up to Jesus' programme for the restoration of God's people. In this, he seems to have lost all that he has been hoping for and everything for which he was following Jesus. His commitment to Jesus as the Messiah seems to have been washed away. He has genuinely lost his way. Where does he go now that Jesus walks towards his crucifixion and Peter has abandoned him on that road? 'For those who want to save their life will lose it' (16:25). Who knows what words of Jesus were echoing in Peter's head, but none of them were likely to do anything other than sharpen Peter's sense of failure and loss. At this moment, Peter has lost his integrity and his tears show recognition of that. But is this the moment that defines Peter? I think not. Peter was restored and, according to Matthew, commissioned to make disciples of all nations (28:16–20).

Like Peter, we all have moments in life – we all have moments in faith – but which are the ones we allow to define us? We will have many moments with God, good and bad, throughout our life of faith, and each one will teach us something new about God and his ways with us. However, it remains vital that we allow ourselves to be defined by God's saving work and not by our failures.

6 Defining moments (2)

Matthew 27:1–10

Sometimes, the gospels juxtapose two stories because the evangelists want us to read these stories together and so see each more clearly in the light of the other. (Think for one moment of the Jewish male leader meeting Jesus by night and not committing to him, followed by the Samaritan woman meeting Jesus by day and understanding Jesus is the Messiah in John 3—4.) Matthew does that rather deftly here with the stories of Peter's denial and Judas' betrayal.

Like Peter, Judas does what Jesus has already predicted he will do (26:25). Like Peter, he comes to regret his action. He goes to the chief priests and elders to give back the money that they paid him to betray Jesus. His words say it all, 'I have sinned by betraying innocent blood' (v. 4). Just as Peter wept bitterly, so Judas throws down the 30 pieces of silver in the temple. Both reach the point of despair, but their stories end very differently. Peter weeps, stays in touch with the disciples and Jesus rehabilitates him. Judas hangs himself.

By putting the stories together, Matthew presents us as the gospel audience with a profound reflection and a choice that those of us who reach the depths of despair will need to make. Despair can move us in very different directions. What if Judas had grieved his evil actions and allowed Jesus' call to repentance to shape his future? We can look at Thomas, who was hardly the model disciple when it came to courageous faith. He allowed his scepticism to speak more loudly than his faith more than once. Yet tradition has it that Thomas took the gospel to India. God can make a missionary out of a repentant sceptic. What region of the world might have owed its salvation to St Judas? Peter became the bishop of Rome, having headed up the mother church in Jerusalem. God can do wonderful things with people who allow themselves to be transformed by his grace.

All this reminds us that the same is true of God today as in the first century AD. The God who worked in them is also at work in us. Let's resist the temptation to be defined by anything other than God's good grace.

66

23–29 October

Guidelines

I want to commend a basic spiritual practice to you. It concerns the way we read the Bible. When we read stories, we may identify with particular characters and read the stories through their eyes. In reality, more often than not we are reading them through our own eyes but are identifying with the character closest to us or to how we would like to see ourselves. In reading the Bible, we may identify with God and, in the gospels, with Jesus. This seems natural, as we seek to follow God. We are disciples of Jesus and would like to think we are becoming like Jesus (and it is our sincere hope and prayer that we are). However, in doing this we can miss much of the poignancy of the biblical message for ourselves.

Jesus speaks to various kinds of broken and sinful people with whom we have quite a lot in common. When we read the stories through Jesus' eyes, we can look down on these characters: what foolish disciples, not understanding Jesus! How hypocritical the Pharisees are! But when we read the stories through the eyes of these characters, suddenly things look different. Reading as the disciples, we may realise that we too have struggled to understand what on earth Jesus is saying at times, as it seems so at odds with our preconceived ideas of life and faith. Hearing Jesus with the Pharisees, we may realise that we too struggle to 'bring in the kingdom' just as they did, and we can find Jesus' critiques of our efforts quite difficult to take. But hearing the gospel stories afresh in our vulnerability as those to whom Jesus speaks (rather than the ivory tower of looking out at those to whom he speaks in the stories) brings us much closer to our living Lord.

Reading the passion story, in particular, becomes infinitely more powerful when we read it through the eyes of the broken and sinful characters. No longer does Peter weep bitterly as we look on disappointedly at his weakness, but we are faced with our own betrayals of Jesus. When we are there, his offer of forgiveness means so much more.

1 The king

Matthew 27:11–31

The power dynamics of this narrative are complex. The chief priests and elders want Jesus killed for blasphemy but have no authority to execute him. They bring Jesus to Pilate and, presumably, accuse him of being a messianic leader. That explains Pilate's question, 'Are you the King of the Jews?' (v. 11). Pilate governs a troublesome province. It borders on enemy territory and has a history of rebellion. So it is a weak spot in the borders of the Roman empire against the mighty Parthians. Consequently, Pilate does not want trouble. First, he is concerned that Jesus might be another rebel leader who sets themselves up as a new Moses or David leading the Jews into political freedom. Hence his question to Jesus. Then he is concerned about a riot turning into a rebellion. Passover was a time when these kinds of riots tended to happen – not surprisingly, as Passover celebrated escaping slavery in Egypt and gaining political freedom. The crowd are manipulated by the chief priests and elders, who have feared their reaction before now, but as Barabbas was probably a revolutionary (Mark 15:7), the crowd would have liked him. The jostling for power to influence what happens to Jesus is a thread that runs through this narrative.

However, the narrative starts and ends by naming Jesus as the king of the Jews (vv. 11, 29). Pilate consistently refers to Jesus as the one who is called the Messiah, understanding Jesus to be a claimant to the throne and the promises of David. Before they take Jesus away to crucify him, they strip him and dress him mockingly as a king. The irony is intense, as throughout the jostling for power, the one who has the authority to call down twelve legions of angels stood among them without grasping for power. When the soldiers mock Jesus as (in their view) another failed 'Davidic Messiah', they mock the one who is not only David's son but his Lord. Jesus exercises his authority in receiving from the Father the cup that the Father has handed him. His struggle was in Gethsemane. He now takes the humiliation, the mockery, the foolishness, the lack of understanding and the rejection – and, as he has said, all to give his life as a ransom for many.

2 The Son of God

Matthew foregrounds the title 'Son of God' in his gospel, and particularly here at the crucifixion. An ancient Jewish text, the Wisdom of Solomon, uses the term 'son of God' to describe the truly righteous person in terms of his enemies lying in wait for him, rejecting his knowledge of God, disliking him for pointing out their sin, and testing him with torture and a shameful death to see if God would rescue him (Wisdom of Solomon 2:12-20). This model 'son of God' (i.e. righteous man) goes through exactly what Jesus suffers. It seems as if Matthew has taken Jesus' life and passion and read them through the lens of the righteous man of the Wisdom of Solomon in order to show both to the early Christians and to the various groups of Jews around at the time that Jesus models true obedience to the Father, as he actually lived out in history exactly what the model righteous person would do. Matthew portrays Jesus the obedient son of God as an example to us all. We are to live as Jesus lived, and we are to be prepared to carry our crosses and give our lives for God just as Jesus did for us.

But another thing is going on in calling Jesus 'Son of God'. The words of the centurion are very little like the equivalent words at Mark 15:39 (very likely Matthew's source). Matthew makes the words of his centurion (v. 54) virtually identical to the words of the disciples when Jesus walks on the sea (14:22-33). Matthew wants us to read the crucifixion in terms of this story. When Jesus walks on the sea, Matthew quotes Job 9:8 to signal that we are to see this as God the divine warrior walking on the back of the defeated mythic enemy, the sea. Thus Matthew paints Jesus as the one who defeats all that the mythic enemy, the sea, stood for: political instability, economic hardship, foreign oppression, injustice in the nation, evil and death – and he did this on the cross, as well as offering himself as a sacrifice for sin (26:26-29). The obedient Son of God offers his life so that we might have life in all its fullness.

3 Drifting away

Matthew 27:55–66

Knowing the joyful ending means I find it hard to fully enter into the first few verses of our reading. One of the noteworthy aspects of our passage is how unadorned it is with references to the Old Testament and wider Jewish culture and literature. The crucifixion is full of such references. We explored only two, but there are references to Psalms 22 and 69, as well as the use of theophanic portents. The text is rich with quotations, allusions and echoes that direct us as the reader deeper and deeper into the text to see all that Matthew would like us to notice and so understand about Jesus and his work on the cross.

But as we enter this next part of the narrative, the text is stripped bare of such allusions. Joseph of Arimathea requests the body of Jesus, possibly because he wants to bury it before the end of the day as required in Deuteronomy 21:22–23, but even here Matthew does not use a single word to allude to that text. After the incredible work of the cross, we are simply left with loss and the continuing drift of disciples.

All the male disciples have now fled. In verse 55, many women are looking on at Jesus' crucifixion from a distance, including the three named Mary. By the time of Jesus' burial, the other women have disappeared and we have only Mary Magdalene and 'the other Mary' watching the internment of Jesus' body. From the ironic heights of the crucifixion with all its rich intertexts, we find ourselves sitting outside the tomb with only two others – and a very large stone rolled across the entrance. To add insult to injury, a guard is put on the tomb to prevent the disciples entering.

Staying with the story at this point is important. There are times of desolation in the life of discipleship. We are not always in the place of Jesus' redemptive suffering or in the place of his victorious resurrection. The same is true of the life of ministry. This was always the case for God's people. How long were they oppressed by the pharaohs? How long were they in exile in Babylon? Sometimes we simply need to stay there, trusting that with God there is always hope.

4 The resurrection

5 The reality of the resurrection

Matthew 28:1-15

Matthew 28:1-10

The portrayal of the resurrection is remarkably understated in the gospel narratives. Our earliest biblical reference to the physical resurrection has the archangel Michael arising to finish off the enemies of the covenant people, a time of anguish and the deliverance of God's people, the resurrection of the dead from their tombs, and a judgement of all (Daniel 12:1–3). Such scenes were depicted in contemporary Jewish texts and often focused on the battle in great detail (like the War Scroll from Qumran) or the glory of God coming with portents in heaven and on earth (like the judgement scene in 1 Enoch 1). Matthew has painted such scenes in the judgement of the nations (e.g. 25:31–46), so he knows of them. Which raises the question: why does Matthew not make more of the resurrection account?

He has filled the crucifixion narrative with quotations, allusions and echoes to the Old Testament and wider Jewish literature and culture. Earlier in his gospel, he has Jesus predict his coming with armies of angels (16:27–28) and with heavenly portents (24:29–31) when he comes as the Son of Man. The Jewish writings of this period understand the resurrection to be part and parcel of the coming of the age to come, the eternal kingdom of God. The word 'resurrection' can act as shorthand for this time. The pictures they paint are generally quite elaborate. So when we see the resurrection from the dead actually happening, why does Matthew not make more of it – especially when we note that Matthew is the only evangelist to describe people rising from the dead when Jesus was crucified (27:52–53)? If he makes this link, which signals that Jesus' death brings life to the people of God, why only an earthquake and one shining angel – and the earthquake to signal the angel's arrival? And why the mildly comic detail of the angel sitting on the stone?

Very likely, Matthew (like his fellow evangelists) wants us to ponder the reality of the event. You only need to read Ezekiel 37 to understand how resurrection scenes could act as symbolism. Matthew leads us to wonder at the fact that this really happened and so to understand that everything the resurrection stands for symbolically also becomes real in Jesus.

5 The reality of the resurrection

Matthew has bracketed the story of the resurrection with this story about the guard being set on the tomb. Framing one story inside another was a literary technique the evangelists borrowed from the literature of contemporary cultures (Mark was very fond of the technique). The idea is that the audience reads the two stories in terms of each other. The story of the guards at the tomb concerns making sure news of the resurrection does not get out. The first part of the story (27:62–66) recounts the chief priests and Pharisees asking Pilate for a guard on the tomb so the disciples cannot steal the body to fake a resurrection and deceive the people with news of Jesus risen from the dead. The second bracket of this story (vv. 11–15) has the chief priests and elders paying off the guards to claim that Jesus' disciples stole the body while they were asleep, with promises of protecting them from possibly severe military discipline. The story is not aimed primarily at denying the resurrection – far from it; the chief priests do not express a single doubt about the soldiers' story. The story concerns their desire to prevent the resurrection story getting out.

The effect of bracketing this around the resurrection is to tell the gospel audience (including ourselves) that the news of Jesus rising from the dead is news that must get out there. This works in three ways. The gospel audience hears that some would suppress this news, and still do today in countries where Christians are persecuted and/or banned from sharing faith in Jesus. Conversely, as a gospel audience we hear that we really ought to be spreading this good news. Finally, this sets us up for the great commission which follows and in which Jesus calls his disciples to make disciples of all nations.

So how do we react? Matthew calls on each and every one of us to share the good news of Jesus' resurrection. For some of us, this is daunting. For others, it is perfectly natural. Wherever we are on the spectrum of willingness, we could all do with praying that Jesus will strengthen us in this ministry. How much would the chief priests need to spend to keep us quiet?

6 Understanding our mission clearly

Matthew 28:16–20

I have found Jesus' words in this text increasingly challenging over the years – particularly since becoming a parish priest. When young, I read them as a call to bring people to faith and, as this seemed quite daunting enough, simply read 'make disciples' as 'share your faith in Jesus and hope somebody accepts what he has done for them on the cross'. I suspect I am not alone in this understanding of mission, as it is one many people embrace and many others react against, often in favour of types of community transformation at home and abroad. But this is not what Jesus says.

Jesus calls us to make disciples, but the command 'make disciples' is grammatically linked to two other actions which spell out what the action of making disciples actually involves. The first is baptising them in the name of the Father, Son and Holy Spirit. As baptism involves repentance (compare Matthew 3), this means bringing people to ask forgiveness of their sins and commit to living righteously, as that is what the Greek word for repentance (*metanoia*) means. The God in whose name we do this is the Father, Son and Holy Spirit, and no other God or understanding of God. This can feel challenging as it involves an exclusive commitment to this one true God, which might be unfashionable in these inclusivist times.

But the bigger challenge comes with the second half of our missional obligation. We are to teach people to obey everything that Jesus has commanded. Matthew has focused throughout his gospel on the theme of discipleship. He has gathered Jesus' teachings into five blocks to mirror the five books of the law, and so to make clear that Jesus gives in his teaching the final interpretation of the law. Jesus gives stern warnings, even to those who deem themselves wonderfully Spirit-filled Christians, to live as he commands (7:21–23). However, he tells us that he is present with us as the one true teacher (23:8), teaching his disciples in gentleness and strength how to live out his commands (11:28–30). The mission may be daunting, but it comes with his promise to be with us constantly as we obey him in making disciples.

Guidelines

If I read the subculture of the church correctly, then the idea of being counter-cultural has grown in its popularity since the 1980s when it may have been a bit edgy in some quarters. I can remember fringe seminars at Christian festivals where we young ones were urged to stand against the tide of culture. Culture was generally defined as individualistic capitalism, and the issues on which we had to stand up were ecological and race issues, with a degree of commitment to closing the gap between the rich and the poor (and these all are good things). In one sense, we have done a great job, as these issues are now out there in the media and whether or not most people do anything about them, few would challenge them publicly as currents of our culture which deserve our support. Although sectors of the church still call these things countercultural, they are now – in reality – actually rather mainstream.

Perhaps those of us who consider ourselves radical (another popular fringe term from the 1980s) could try the gospel of Matthew. If anything in Christian faith is countercultural at the moment, then it is the great commission (Matthew 28:18–20). It contains five words that are almost guaranteed to make the average 1980s radically countercultural Christian guru spit, as they cut right across our assumption that we have a right to autonomy and public self-expression. These five dirty words are authority, teach, obey, command and judgement. So much radical Christianity seems to adopt a liberationist reading of Paul, where freedom from the law is interpreted as freedom from any requirement to follow any ethic, that Jesus can come as quite a shock. But Jesus is and always has been radical. He takes us right back to the roots of faith, which always were and always will be total surrender to God in worship and complete obedience, knowing his grace and love in saving us from sin, death and the devil – and it is here that we truly find life in him. To be honest, that is now the only kind of radicalism I desire.

FURTHER READING

Andy Angel, *The Jesus You Really Didn't Know: Rediscovering the teaching ministry of Jesus* (Cascade, 2019).

R. T. France, *The Gospel of Matthew (The New International Commentary on the New Testament)* (Eerdmans, 2007).

N. T. Wright, *Surprised by Hope: Rethinking heaven, the resurrection and the mission of the church* (SPCK, 2011).

Images of the church in the New Testament

Helen Miller

March 2020 likely sticks in our memories. It saw the first UK lockdown in response to the Covid-19 pandemic, with schools, businesses and churches adopting online forums to continue their work. Reflection on the pandemic has prompted questions about church. Should live-streaming be part of the new normal? Why have some churches kept people connected better than others? What is the role of the church in wider society and how is this best achieved? Addressing these and other such questions requires an understanding of the nature and role of the church. 'What is the church?' is one way that we might phrase our enquiry. John Stackhouse encourages us to frame our search differently, asking not, 'What is the church?', but 'Who and whose is the church?' (Stackhouse, p. 9).

Swapping 'what' for 'who and whose' is affirmed by the New Testament, which focuses less on institutional structures and more on the identity and work of the triune God upon whom the church is founded. One of the ways that the relationship between the church and the Trinity is conveyed is through images. Paul Minear argues that there are over 80 such images, including salt, light, vine branches, a vineyard, wearers of white robes and an olive. These images don't depict different churches but highlight particular aspects of *the* church as a singular entity, albeit one that has multiple expressions through time and across the globe. We'll focus on six of these images: people of God, temple of the Holy Spirit, body of Christ, new creation, bride of Christ and family. We'll explore what light these images shed on the nature and role of the church, in particular who and whose it is.

Unless otherwise stated, Bible quotations are taken from the NRSV.

1 People of God

Genesis 12:1–3; Ephesians 2:1–18

When did the church begin? Minear argues that the church's origin is not Pentecost, the great commission or even Jesus' birth. Rather, the church is the people of God whose covenantal relationship with God begins with Abraham (Minear, p. 70). When Abraham first appears, the situation is looking bleak. The spiral of sin seems in continual descent. But God has other plans. He promises that, through Abraham, 'all the families of the earth shall be blessed' (Genesis 12:3). Partial fulfilment occurs as 'a mixed crowd' joins the Israelites in their exodus from Egypt (Exodus 12:38) and as foreigners such as Ruth and Rahab are brought into the line of blessing (Matthew 1:5). Jesus' call to his followers to 'make disciples of all nations' reveals the fulfilment of God's promise through Jesus' work, as is beautifully portrayed in John's description of 'a great multitude that no one could count, from every nation, from all tribes and peoples and languages, standing before the throne and before the Lamb' (Revelation 7:9).

The fulfilment of God's promise is also evident in Ephesians 2. Paul celebrates that those who were 'far off' (v. 13) and 'aliens from the commonwealth of Israel, and strangers to the covenants of promise' (v. 12) have become God's people through Jesus' work. This is no small change in identity but a move from death to life, from facing God's wrath to receiving his mercy, and from servitude to desire to service to Christ. It is also through Jesus that Jewish believers, 'those who were near', have access to the Father, and one church is formed from those who were formerly enemies (v. 14).

The people of God image encourages the church to discover its identity and purpose from all of scripture, while noting the fulfilment of the Old Testament in Christ. To encourage us in this, Tom Wright gives the example of a Shakespearian play whose fifth act has been lost. He notes that skilled actors could improvise the fifth act so long as they'd immersed themselves in the first four acts to learn the nature of the play and its characters. Likewise, he argues, the church is to so immerse itself in scripture that it can live out of this story in ways that are faithful to God, scripture's author (see Wright, *The New Testament and the People of God*).

2 Temple of the Holy Spirit

Is the church perfect or imperfect? A glance at the church in history and today makes the answer clear: the church is imperfect. It consists of broken people who have been rescued and redeemed but are still works in progress. Such is the church's imperfection that it isn't uncommon to meet people who, while still claiming faith in Jesus, struggle hugely with his church.

However, while the church's faults are self-evident, the New Testament reveals that the question of the church's perfection is complex. On the one hand, people like Paul were painfully aware of problems in the churches to whom they wrote. If you're discouraged by your own church, read 1 Corinthians and you'll see that struggling churches are nothing new. And yet, on the other hand, because of the forgiveness and transformation achieved through Jesus' death and resurrection, the Corinthian Christians are described as 'sanctified in Christ Jesus' and 'called to be his holy people' (1 Corinthians 1:2, NIV). In addition, the church doesn't exist as an independent and autonomous entity. Its life is founded on and sustained by the work of the triune God, who is resplendent in holiness and perfection.

The church's dependence on God is highlighted by the image of the church as a temple of the Spirit. To understand the power of this imagery, we need to see the temple's significance earlier in scripture. As Genesis 2 reveals, there isn't a temple in Eden. Rather, the garden itself is the temple – a place of intimacy with God. Prior to their rebellion against God, Adam and Eve relate to God without fear. However, when sin distorts humans' relationship with God, in his grace God provides the sacrificial system and tabernacle (then temple) so that his people can still meet with him. There are strict limits on this access, though. Entry to the Most Holy Place, where God's presence dwelt in its most intimate tangibility, was restricted to one man, the high priest, on one day of the year, the Day of Atonement. In Ephesians 2, therefore, Paul marvels that, through Jesus, it isn't just that all God's people can access the most intimate part of God's temple, but that they themselves have become this temple. The challenge is to live accordingly, allowing the resplendent perfection of Christ's Spirit to shine through our words and deeds.

3 Body of Christ

What does a healthy church look like? The church in Corinth provides a sobering counter-example. Sexual immorality, greed, pride and selfishness are problems in the community. And yet, for all the character flaws on display, God has been generous with the gifts he's bestowed. Paul highlights the Corinthian church's richness of knowledge and observes no lack of spiritual gifts among them (1 Corinthians 1:5–7). This outpouring of gifts is significant in the overarching story of scripture. In the Old Testament, the Spirit empowers people for particular tasks, such as authoritative speech (e.g. 2 Samuel 23:2; Micah 3:8) and leadership (e.g. Numbers 27:18). However, the infilling presence of the Spirit for all God's people, and the bestowal of all with spiritual gifts, is something that the Old Testament prophets look forward to in hope (Joel 2:28–32; Ezekiel 36:25–27).

The gift of God's Spirit is now poured out on all God's people as a result of Jesus' death, resurrection and ascension. Different gifts are given to different people, which can lead to comparison and jealousy. Paul adopts and adapts the metaphor of a body, which was used to encourage unity in the wider Roman world, to help his readers see their mutual interdependence.

For Paul, though, the church is not just a body; it is Christ's body. Jesus' nature and work is the foundation for believers' relationships with each other, marking the church out as distinctively countercultural. For example, whereas Greco-Roman moralists used the body metaphor to maintain pre-established hierarchies, Paul's body of Christ image turns the Corinthian Christians' hierarchical schemas on their head. It is not those who already receive honour who need more but those who lack it (1 Corinthians 12:23–24). The seemingly weaker members are those Paul highlights as being indispensable (1 Corinthians 12:22).

In addition, the key issue for Paul is not what gifts people have but whether they use them with humility as a blessing to others, or out of pride for their own selfish gain. As Paul goes on to argue, the health of a church is not ascertained by the quantity of its gifting but the quality of its love (1 Corinthians 13). We don't achieve this in our own strength. Remarkable intimacy between Christ and his church is conveyed through the depiction of the church as his body. It is Christ's presence in our lives that enables us to love and bless others.

4 New creation

How does the church grow? When we reflect on the salvation that we receive through Jesus' sacrifice, we are inspired to share this good news with others. Passion for people to know Jesus as Saviour and Lord should characterise the church. However, a healthy desire to share the gospel with others can be replaced by an anxious striving for congregational growth to attain prestige and worldly success. Glen Scrivener compares this unhealthy striving with Jesus' example. He writes:

Jesus never suffered from anxiety about the size or prospects of his movement. In Matthew 5 his band of followers was small and unimpressive, and his shameful death was imminent, but his belief in global success was unshakeable. Christ's concern was not so much that his church grow (he knew it would do that); he was concerned that it be distinct.

Glen Scrivener, *The Air We Breathe: How we all came to believe in freedom, kindness, progress, and equality* (The Good Book Company, 2022), p. 194

Distinctiveness is a key theme in Colossians 3. Paul urges his readers to put on their 'new self' and outlines what this looks like in practice. The transition from the old to the new self is so significant that Paul describes the old self as dead. Ezekiel prophesises this same reality through recording God's promise to remove people's hearts of stone and give them a new heart that is filled with God's Spirit (Ezekiel 36:26–27). Paul sees that this promised transformation has been achieved through Jesus. Christians' union with Jesus means that, just as they share in his death, so they are raised with Christ as new creations.

This identity as a new creation is the reality of all Christians. However, Paul urges his readers to walk more fully in this reality through directing their thoughts towards Christ, putting to death the corrupt behaviours of the old self and putting on the Christlike characteristics of the new self. Paul's exhortation is: this is who you are, now live it! Living as a new creation isn't a solo endeavour. Paul urges believers to encourage and challenge one another and, with gratitude, sing together songs of praise to God. Encouraging one another to live out our new identities in Christ more fully will help the church grow in Christlikeness. As Scrivener notes in the quote above, it will also help the church grow.

5 Bride of Christ

2 Corinthians 11:1–4; Revelation 21

What are the church's anchors? As Paul emphasises, a faithful church is anchored to the good news of Jesus, as preached by Jesus' first witnesses and recorded in scripture (2 Corinthians 11:1–4). If a different Jesus is preached than the Jesus whom scripture reveals, it isn't Jesus at all, but a deception. Therefore, as churches adapt to the opportunities and challenges of their context, they must stay anchored to the past events of Jesus' life, death, resurrection and ascension to remain faithful. A key component of the gospel, however, is yet to be realised. Alongside being anchored to the past, churches must also be fastened to the future hope of Jesus' return.

The imagery of the church as Christ's bride depicts the church's future hope, alongside its current reality. This bridal imagery develops the marital metaphor that's used in the Old Testament to describe God's relationship with his people. In the Old Testament, the marital metaphor is predominantly used negatively to depict the rebellion of God's people as an unfaithful wife. These are deeply provocative passages that preachers need to handle with care. In the New Testament, the bridal imagery is used positively to depict the intimacy of relationship between Jesus and his church, although 2 Corinthians 11 echoes the Old Testament in emphasising the importance of faithfulness.

The bridal image is fulfilled in Revelation 21, where the church is described as 'a bride adorned for her husband' (Revelation 21:2). Interestingly, though, when John sees Christ's bride, rather than a beautifully dressed woman, he sees a giant gold cube (Revelation 21:16)! Why this contrast? John's vision mixes metaphors. In describing a cube, John brings to mind not just the temple but a particular part of it, the Most Holy Place. Whereas in the old covenant, only one man could enter the Most Holy Place on one day of the year, when Jesus' returns, the Most Holy Place will fill all of God's creation.

In the busyness and concerns of everyday life, it is easy to get bogged down in the here and now and lose track of where we're going. The bridal imagery encourages us to look ahead to the glorious future that awaits Christ's return: a time when God himself is with his people, wiping every tear from their eyes, and when death, mourning, crying and pain are no more (Revelation 21:3–4).

6 Family

Isaiah 11:1–9; Ephesians 6:10–24

In Ephesians 6, Paul draws on a military metaphor to encourage his readers to stand against the devil's schemes. Paul was probably influenced in his armour metaphor by the soldiers of his day. He also draws on Old Testament imagery. In Isaiah 11:5, the prophesied Messiah is described wearing righteousness and faithfulness as a belt. In Isaiah 59:17, God puts on righteousness as a breastplate and a helmet of salvation on his head. In both verses, the context is God's victory in bringing judgement on those who oppose him and salvation for those who repent.

In Ephesians, God's victory is a strong theme. Jesus is victorious over sin, death and the devil through his death and resurrection. Putting on the spiritual armour helps us stand firm in this victory. However, the different pieces of armour are not standalone commodities. We don't put on truth, faith or salvation as separate items. Rather, through our union with Jesus, his righteousness becomes our righteousness and his inheritance becomes our salvation. To put on God's armour is to put on Jesus, the ultimate victor, himself. Prayer is important in this. Paul instructs us to pray and in particular to pray 'for all the saints' (Ephesians 6:18). If Paul were to draw again on a military metaphor here, he could have turned to the Roman army's tortoise formation. A single soldier was vulnerable to attack, as their shield only covered part of their body. In the tortoise formation, soldiers stood close together, encasing the whole group in an impenetrable wall of shields, in front, at the sides and above.

Paul closes Ephesians with a blessing for all the brothers and sisters (Ephesians 6:23). This is just one example of how the language of brothers and sisters, and therefore the image of church as a family, pervades the New Testament. As with the Roman soldier, it is hard, even impossible, to stand alone. Rather, as brothers and sisters together in Christ, we are called to stand together. 'Two are better than one… For if they fall, one will lift up the other; but woe to one who is alone and falls and does not have another to help' (Ecclesiastes 4:9–10). As we commit to our local churches, let us ensure that neither we, nor anyone else in our community, stands or falls alone.

Guidelines

When the church is confused about who it is and whose it is, it can become just another institution, just another collective, just another voluntary society… We need ecclesiology so that we can be who and whose we truly are.

Stackhouse, p. 9

When we think about church, it is easy to go straight to issues of format and structure. What should Sunday services look like? What leadership styles and structures are most faithful to scripture? How formal or informal should the relationship between churches be? How often should Communion be undertaken and in what format? How do we best bear witness to Jesus within our local community? These are crucial questions. However, we're best placed to address these important issues if we have a robust understanding of the nature and role of church.

As we've considered who and whose the church is, my hope is that we've been encouraged and inspired by the images we've looked at. What an amazing privilege that the church is the temple of God's Spirit, the place where God's presence is experienced in its greatest tangibility. How awe-inspiring that the relationship between Jesus and his church is so intimate that the church is described as his body and bride. How mind-blowing that the church experiences the fulfilment of promises made over 4,000 years ago. What a blessing that we're not asked to walk the Christian life alone but that we do so empowered by Jesus' presence in our lives and in fellowship with brothers and sisters who stand alongside us. What incredible hope that the church will one day be the perfected bride of Christ, dwelling in the new heavens and new earth, where sin, death and pain are no more.

As you continue to reflect on the nature and role of the church, consider the following questions:

- Which of the images we've looked at has challenged and/or encouraged you the most? Why?
- What other images of the church in the New Testament are you aware of and what light do they shed on the nature and role of the church?

FURTHER READING

Gene L. Green, Stephen T. Pardue and K. K. Yeo (eds), *The Church from Every Tribe and Tongue: Ecclesiology in the majority world* (Langham Creative Projects, 2018) – available as part 5 of: Green, Pardue and Yeo (eds), *Majority World Theology: Christian doctrine in global context* (InterVarsity Press, 2020).

Tim Keller, *Center Church: Doing balanced, gospel-centred ministry in your city* (Zondervan, 2012).

Grace Ji-Sun Kim and Graham Hill, *Healing Our Broken Humanity: Practices for revitalizing the church and renewing the world* (IVP, 2018).

Paul S. Minear, *Images of the Church in the New Testament* (Westminster John Knox, 2004).

Helen Morris, *Flexible Church: Being the church in the contemporary world* (SCM Press, 2019).

John G. Stackhouse Jr (ed.), *Evangelical Ecclesiology: Reality or illusion?* (Baker Academic, 2003).

N. T. Wright, *The New Testament and the People of God* (SPCK, 1992).

Romans 13—16: riding with Romans

Stephen Finamore

In the earlier chapters of his letter, Paul set out his understanding of what God has accomplished through sending his Son into the world. Chapter 12 saw Paul begin to explore the implications of this for his audiences in the different house churches in Rome. The next two chapters – and a bit of the one after – continue this exploration of Christian ethics as the apostle reflects on issues that he is aware of in Rome and offers his views on how people should live and relate to one another, and to wider society, in the light of the gospel.

Then Paul gives us some remarkable insights into his own personal thinking. We read about his sense that a particular stage of ministry has finished and that a new one is about to begin. We see his commitment to visiting Jerusalem even though it may mean he faces danger. And we see his desire to visit the churches in Rome and then go on to proclaim the gospel in Spain.

In the last chapter, we get a sense of the extensive network of relationships he already has in the city as the names of those he knows, knows of and prays for pour out. Finally, we get an astonishing doxology that offers a kind of summing up of Paul's message.

Unless otherwise stated, Bible quotations are taken from the NRSV.

1 Recognising the state

Romans 13:1–7

Paul knows all too well that Rome's Jewish community has had an uneasy relationship with the government. This was a community that refused to honour the local gods and who had customs that set them apart from their neighbours. It thus might be unwise of them to draw any further attention to themselves. But this is exactly what had happened a few years before Paul wrote, when they allowed internal disagreements about 'Chrestus' – probably a reference to arguments about whether Jesus of Nazareth was the Christ, the Messiah – to spill out into public disputes, which may have involved disturbances about conflicting claims to property such as synagogue buildings. The upshot was that all the Jews, Christian and non-Christian, were expelled from Rome (Luke refers to this in Acts 18:2). The last thing they needed was anything like this happening again. This may be why Paul takes such a strong line on accepting the authority of the state: 'Let every person be subject to the governing authorities; for there is no authority except from God, and those authorities that exist have been instituted by God' (v. 1).

The state, we learn, has a God-given purpose that deserves our respect: 'Whoever rebels against the authority is rebelling against what God has instituted' (v. 2). That purpose includes operating a judicial system motivated by 'wrath' which, in this context, appears to mean a strong commitment to ensuring that justice is done by approving what is good and punishing that which is bad. Nero was emperor when these words were written, and Paul does not explore what our attitude might be when the state does things that oppose its own true purpose, something which may have happened when Nero launched his fierce persecution of the church. Perhaps Paul would insist that honouring God must come before any honour owed to the state and that in such difficult circumstances different advice would need to be given.

2 The debt we all owe

Paul has just spoken about the need to pay taxes when they are due ('Pay to all what is due to them – taxes to whom taxes are due, revenue to whom revenue is due, respect to whom respect is due, honour to whom honour is due', 8:7). Here, he expands on the point; all debts are to be paid. In other words, all disputes ought to be avoided. The only debt or obligation that should remain is the continuing one to love. This is certainly a responsibility that those in the churches owe to one another, but in the context it seems to extend beyond the church to become something owed to the rest of society as well.

Paul is clearly drawing on his understanding of the teaching of Jesus as the one who comes to fulfil the law (Matthew 5:17). The apostle understands that the goal of the law is love and that those who love are keeping the essence of the law and are in line with its true purpose. If you love, then you do not murder, you do not covet and so on. The reason that you do not do these things is that the well-being of others matters to you as much as your own well-being. Therefore, if we love, then we do not do some categories of things the law forbids. Indeed, we live the kind of life that the law was intended to promote. Jesus' purpose was to fulfil the law, and this is accomplished when those who follow him love their neighbours as themselves.

For the churches, the communities of followers of Jesus, love is the measure of all things. And the faithfulness to the point of death of Messiah Jesus is the measure of love. Paul's words challenge us all to examine ourselves to see how we measure up.

3 What time is it?

Paul's teaching about the way the followers of Jesus should live has several foundations, including the teaching of Jesus that Paul so often echoes, the work of the Spirit that transforms people from within, and the recognition that certain behaviour is appropriate for those who belong to the Messiah. Supplementing all of these is Paul's insistence that *the time we live in* demands a certain way of life. Just as Jesus calls for people to change their way of living because the kingdom of God is drawing near, Paul calls on Jesus' followers to maintain their commitment because ultimate salvation is drawing ever closer.

Paul makes his point using the illustration of night and day. In the night, people may be sleeping or they may be using the cover of darkness to engage in disreputable behaviour. When day draws near, it is time to wake up or time to behave differently. This chimes well with the teaching of Jesus that his followers should stay alert. The idea is that the people of God should always be on their toes: like an army always ready for an inspection or a battalion always prepared for deployment. All inappropriate behaviour should be jettisoned, and lives should be modelled on Jesus. He is the uniform that this army wears. Paul tells the Roman churches that they know what time it is. It is the time when the kingdom is about to dawn, the time when the light of God is about to break in. The followers of Jesus should know the time. And should live accordingly.

The *Bulletin of Atomic Scientists* publishes the well-known Doomsday Clock, which purports to show how far away the world is from global catastrophe. At the time of writing, they claim we are 90 seeconds away from midnight. They want to draw our attention to the dangers we face and encourage us to change our behaviour. Paul's idea might suggest a similar clock, but his is ticking towards daybreak. It's worth thinking about which of these clocks has the greater power to enable real change.

4 'Weak' and 'strong'

There were lots of divisions within the Roman churches, and one that had come to Paul's notice was between two parties whom somebody had tagged the 'weak' and the 'strong'. In some ways this is a practical outworking on a specific issue of the general advice he has just given to offer love to your neighbour and to avoid quarrelling. Paul's advice starts at the beginning of chapter 14 and continues into the opening verses of chapter 15, where it blends into a discussion about Jews and Gentiles. This suggests that one of the groups consisted mainly of Jewish Christians, perhaps with a few sympathetic Gentile Christians, including some who were connected to the synagogues before they heard about Jesus. This also implies that the other group were mainly Gentile. Almost certainly the 'weak' group, concerned about meat that might have been sacrificed to a pagan god, thereby linking it to idolatry, and about marking certain feast days, was mainly Jewish, while the 'strong' was largely Gentile.

Paul is determined to act as a mediator between the two. His main plea is that the two groups should welcome one another and that they shouldn't argue over things that Paul plainly regards as secondary issues. It appears that the two groups, or perhaps some representatives of each, were inclined to despise and judge the others. Paul's point is that all those involved had been welcomed by God and therefore should welcome one another. Each was a servant of God and should leave any issues of judgement to their master. And God would ensure that any judgement would be favourable.

In times like our own, when people are anxious about the things that are going on in international relations, national government and the economy, it is very easy to lose perspective and to treat secondary issues as though they were of vital importance. Paul's guidance may be just what we need right now.

5 Whose are you?

Paul drives home his point by reminding his readers to whom they belong and therefore for whom they live. If some people want to keep a festival and do so to honour God, why would anyone else want to argue about it? If those who eat all kinds of food do so with gratitude to God, then nobody else should object. After all, Jesus is the Lord of everything. It's not our place to pass judgement on anyone else in the church. And it's not at all appropriate to look down our noses at other Christians. God is the judge, and we are not.

Some have wondered whether Paul's openness on these issues stands in contrast to things he says elsewhere, such as his objection to those promoting male circumcision of Gentile Christians in Galatia. Perhaps the difference is that in Galatia Paul's opponents seem to have been arguing that circumcision was a requirement for a male to be counted as part of the people of God. Paul regarded that message as a false gospel. The issues were different in Rome, and Paul could be an advocate of unity. This does not mean that there were no issues that would lead Paul to call for church discipline. The key is to know which things can be done in a way that honours God and which cannot. The things that Paul criticised included the proclamation of a false gospel and sexual immorality. However, he was quite content to accept people who held that some days were special or had a kind of 'don't ask, don't tell' policy regarding the sources of their food.

Some argue that the categories 'weak' and 'strong' betray Paul's own convictions, but this is not necessarily the case. It is certainly true that Paul, even though he was a Jewish Christian, might have been sympathetic with the arguments of the 'strong'. Nevertheless, his desire to be a peacemaker makes it unlikely that he invented the categories, and it seems more likely that he was adopting the language used by one of the groups – probably 'the strong' – about the other. This is certainly the group that he addresses first in his discussion.

It may be worth thinking through how Paul's discussion should influence any discussions or disputes that we find ourselves involved in. Do we find ourselves counted among the 'weak' or the 'strong'? And how do we feel when others use these labels to define us?

6 The call to mutual upbuilding

One of the issues with all the quarrelling going on within and between the Roman house churches is that people were interfering with one another's discipleship. They were like runners from the same team who, instead of helping one another, were digging holes or putting barriers in one another's paths. Paul knew that Jesus had declared all foods to be clean. Often, it's not that things are wrong in themselves so much as the way in which we do them that causes problems. In the end, the test is love. If something we do is harming the discipleship of another, then it is not a loving thing to do. After all, Jesus loved them enough to die for them, so why would we want to bring them to ruin?

Paul thought that the Roman churches needed to sort out their priorities. Their goal should have been the kingdom of God and the kingdom is righteousness, peace and joy, not everyday eating and drinking. Another way to look at the issue is through the lens of service. If we are serving Jesus, then our brothers and sisters should support us and not judge us.

Paul had a passion for unity: 'Let us then pursue what makes for peace and for mutual edification' (v. 19). He believed that God was building the church. It is the task of Christians to join in with that, not to undermine it. Especially not for something as irrelevant as which food you choose to eat. The focus should not be on arguments about food or special days but on the impact of our behaviour on fellow followers of Jesus. The key question is whether a position helps or harms others. Does it undermine or edify the church? After that, what matters is your own conviction. If your behaviour is an expression of your faith, then it is fine. If not, then it needs to be reconsidered.

Guidelines

Paul is continuing to set out all the implications of his earlier theological arguments. After discussing the role of the state, he mentions two foundational ideas in his ethics. The first of these is love as the thing that fulfils God's purposes for us. The second is the idea that this has become urgent because we live at a time when God's light could burst in at any moment. Next, Paul thinks about the tensions that existed between two groups and that might lead to disunity. Paul makes it clear that there are some things that are not worth quarrelling over. Those who follow Jesus should support and encourage one another, so they must not despise and judge one another. Paul makes it clear that those who belong to God are to build up the things that he is building and love those for whom Jesus died.

- In Romans 13, Paul offers a positive view of the state, which is at odds with the view taken by Revelation. How should the two be reconciled? When is the point reached when the church should cease to obey the state?

- Paul speaks of fulfilling the law at 13:8, but elsewhere he can be understood to argue that the law has fulfilled its purpose (10:4; Galatians 3:23–25). What part, if any, does the law continue to play in God's purposes?

- In Romans 14, Paul seems to regard eating meat as a matter of indifference. The rise, in our own day, of vegetarianism and veganism, sometimes embraced for ethical reasons, means that many think these are issues of great consequence. Is Paul's argument relevant to these matters or has the situation changed so much that his position is out of date?

- Can Paul's position be used by people with certain scruples to manipulate others into changing their practices out of love for their 'weaker' brothers and sisters?

- Paul is capable of arguing that some issues are so significant that those who disagree with him are to be cursed (Galatians 1:8–9) but also of insisting, as he does in Romans 14, that other matters that some regard as important enough to quarrel about are in fact issues on which different views can be legitimately held. Is there an 'acid' test for knowing which issues are so important that they provide a justification for disunity?

- Finally, some wonder if Paul, in addition to caring about the unity of the church in Rome for its own sake, also wanted the church to unite so that it could offer effective support for his proposed mission to Spain. Might this be one of the reasons for his stress on unity?

1 The unity of the people of God is the fulfilment of prophecy

Romans 15:1–13

Here, Paul draws together the threads from his discussion in the preceding chapter. He reiterates his teaching in 14:1 to indicate that he is winding up this part of his argument. The 'strong' must care for the 'weak' and everyone should be concerned for building up their brothers and sisters. As he so often does, Paul points to the example of Messiah Jesus, for he was one who looked to the interests of others. The first half of Psalm 69:9 says, 'It is zeal for your house that has consumed me,' and is used in John's gospel (2:17) in the context of Jesus's action in the temple. Here, in verse 3, Paul cites the second half of the verse, suggesting that the house in question can be understood as the people of God and that the insults we throw at one another fall on Jesus.

Then, in what might appear to be a throwaway line, Paul says something very interesting about the way he understands the Hebrew Bible. Its words are written to instruct the church and to give it hope. Paul sums up this part of the letter with a prayer that God might enable his people to live in harmony with one another. This is not for their own sake but so that they might be united in giving glory to God, which is one of the ways that Paul expresses the ultimate purpose of the whole of creation.

Paul then states the guiding principle for the unity of the church – we should welcome one another just as we have been welcomed by Messiah Jesus, because this will glorify God. He then slips out of the language of the 'weak' and the 'strong' and back into the language of Jew and Gentile. It becomes clear that one of Paul's goals is that these groups should be united as the one people of God. The Messiah served the Jews by confirming the promises made to their physical ancestors with the end purpose of enabling the non-Jewish peoples of the world to give glory to God. Paul offers a string of texts that demonstrate that this was always God's purpose and that the unity of Jew and Gentile is the fulfilment of prophecy. The verses are drawn from all three sections of the Hebrew Bible – the law, the prophets and the writings – for Paul regards this as God's great goal.

It may be worth thinking through whether we think Paul's approach to using the scriptures should guide all our interpretation of them.

2 Paul sums up his letter and his ministry to date

Romans 15:14–21

Paul explains that he has been called by God to be Messiah Jesus' ambassador to the nations of the earth. It is in that capacity that he has felt able to write so boldly to a church that he has never visited. Interestingly, Paul continues to use temple imagery describing his apostolic work as 'priestly' and calling the Gentile followers of Jesus an 'offering'.

He goes on to say some things about the way he carried out this ministry. It was one of word and deed. There are sometimes discussions in certain circles about the relationship between evangelism and social action, between our words and our actions. The apostle seems to see them as one. Here he speaks of signs, wonders and proclamation. Later he will talk about the offering he has taken up for the poor in Jerusalem.

He then makes a startling claim – that he has fully proclaimed the gospel from the Holy Land to what we would now call the Balkans. He may not mean that everyone living in that region had heard the gospel but that churches had been planted in enough strategic locations for his work in the area to be regarded as completed. However, Paul was not considering retirement but was actively planning the next stage of his mission. He would continue to proclaim the gospel of the fulfilment of God's ancient promises, but he would do it somewhere that nobody had yet heard the message.

Paul understood himself as an apostle and as a pioneer. He was what is (or was) known in some circles as a 'fresh-fields evangelist'. His role was to start things from scratch rather than to supplement what others had already begun. The text Paul uses from Isaiah 52:15 is from one of the so-called Servant Songs. Most Christian interpretations of the songs understand them to be about Jesus, but here the apostle understands his own ministry in the light of these words.

Paul had a clear idea of his own calling and could put it into words. How might you express in a few words the tasks or way of life to which you feel called?

3 The grand plan: Spain via Jerusalem and Rome!

Romans 15:22–33

Paul comes full circle and repeats things he said at the start of the letter about his desire to visit Rome. It has not been possible yet because Paul had still to complete the work in his current region. But that is now done, and the apostle is happy to share his plans for the next stage. His ultimate goal is Spain, and he plans to visit Rome on his way there. He even expresses the hope that he might be 'sent on' by the Romans. It is possible that Paul hopes that the churches in Rome, duly united after absorbing his letter and committed to the project after his visit to them, might become a kind of base of operations for his work in Spain, just as the church in Antioch had played that role for his work in the east.

However, before any of that could happen, Paul had a promise to keep. Perhaps it related to the undertaking to remember the poor that he had given to the church leaders in Jerusalem on one of his visits there (Galatians 2:10). In any event, Paul had been gathering a collection for the poor in Jerusalem from among the Gentile churches. He refers to it in both his letters to Corinth (1 Corinthians 16:1–4; 2 Corinthians 8—9; see also the reference to alms in Acts 24:17). Paul regards the offering as a reciprocal gesture – a material blessing from the nations for the spiritual blessings they had received from Jerusalem. The apostle feels an obligation to complete and to deliver the collection before he embarks on the next leg of his ministry.

Paul is aware, however, that he is not popular with everyone in Judea and that the visit to Jerusalem will be fraught with problems. Those who were not Christians might act against him, and even those who followed Jesus might find it difficult to accept his gifts or his ministry. As we know from Acts 21:7—23:30, Paul was right to be concerned. Luke does not explicitly mention the offering in his account. Understandably, the apostle asked the Christians in Rome to join him in earnest prayer for the visit. God, as we know, had different plans. Paul got to Jerusalem and then, according to Acts, was a prisoner when he finally made it to Rome. So far as we know, he never made it to Spain. Even an apostle's seemingly vital plans are subject to being overruled by God.

It is worth thinking through how God can overrule even the best and most inspired of plans. Some of us have personal experience of this and it can be both a painful thing and a powerful lesson.

4 Greetings!

For someone who had never visited Rome, Paul certainly knew a lot of people there. However, before he gets to them, he introduces Phoebe. Almost certainly, she was the one who carried the letter to Rome. Given Paul's warm words, it seems likely that she would be expected to take the letter around the different churches and perhaps help them to understand it by answering questions and even explaining some of the trickier sections.

The first to be greeted are Prisca and Aquila, who get a warm commendation. We know a little about them from Acts 18. One of the churches met in their home, and the fact that Prisca's name is the first to be mentioned suggests that she was the main leader. Almost certainly, many of the others mentioned are leaders of different house churches. Of particular interest is Junia, who is mentioned in verse 7. She had become a Christian before Paul and is described as 'prominent among the apostles'. The place of Phoebe, Prisca, Mary and Junia in the greetings hints at the extent of female leadership in the earliest days of the church.

With one or two exceptions, the people on the list are probably Jewish Christians or those the authorities thought had strong connections with them and who had been exiled from Rome but had now returned. Paul, or one of his team, had probably met them in the course of their mission work. Of course, not all the names are obviously Jewish but lots of members of the Jewish community in Rome were known by Roman names. All these people were probably the hosts and/or the leaders of different churches. One or two of them have names that indicate they were slaves, and this tells us significant things about the church and its leadership.

The list ends with two interesting things. Paul calls on the Christians in Rome to greet one another with a holy kiss. The kiss is a symbol of their unity and mutual belonging. And he sends them the greetings of the other churches, making it clear that they belong to a family of communities that stretched well beyond Rome. We are called to love our local communities and the wider networks of which we are a part.

5 A warning and an introduction to the team

Romans 16:17–23

It almost seemed like the letter had finished, but Paul still has a final warning to issue. Churches he had founded in Galatia and Corinth had been troubled by people who seemed to want to undermine Paul and undo all the work he had done. It is possible that such teachers had now targeted Rome. Paul probably felt that he had no choice but to interrupt the flow of his greetings to issue this warning. The church must always be vigilant to ensure that false teachings do not gain a foothold.

In verse 20, the apostle ends this short section with an assurance that seems to be drawn from the promise to Eve in Genesis 3:15. We usually understand this as a promise of the Messiah who will defeat the enemy, but here Paul sees the church, the body of Messiah Jesus, experiencing God crushing Satan under their feet.

Once the warning is given, Paul goes back to the second part of his greetings, this time introducing the team that has been with him, probably in Corinth, while he wrote the letter. The church, or one of the house churches, met in the home of Gaius and it was there that Paul had received hospitality for his stay. Tertius gets to write his own greeting because he is the one with the stylus. He has had the task of writing down all the things that Paul has wanted to say. There was no straightforward way to make corrections and no editing tools or erasers were available. There were certainly no cut-and-paste facilities. Tertius had to get it right, and so his was a vital role.

Paul valued all the team, including the ones who carried out the vital tasks that happen behind the scenes. It's a good idea to express appreciation regularly for those whose efforts facilitate the more public ministries of others.

6 Closing doxology

The letter ends with a beautiful song of praise to God. Many people wonder whether this is really Paul's intended ending to the letter. Some of them point out that the letter has several apparent endings. Romans 11:36 reads like a conclusion and so does 15:13. The same could be said of 15:33, 16:16 and 16:20. Perhaps these words were added by a later writer. After all, if the heart of the letter is the idea of justification by faith, as so many have insisted, then, surely, you'd expect a reference to this in something that reads as though it might be a summary. On the other hand, if Paul's great central theme is really about the surprising way that God has kept his ancient promises so that the non-Jewish peoples of the world can become a part of the people of God, then perhaps these words are a great way to sum up the whole letter.

There are a number of things that echo thoughts found elsewhere. Paul speaks of 'my gospel' in 2:16. There are several mentions of God revealing things, including his righteousness at 1:17. Paul mentions the mystery of God's purposes in relation to Israel at 11:25, and there are references to prophecy throughout the letter, especially those that concern the promises that the Gentiles will become part of the people of God. Finally, the apostle mentions 'the obedience of faith' as the goal of his work at 1:5. There may be other connections with the case made in the letter. As we draw towards the end of our study, it would be a useful exercise to consider how you might summarise Paul's overall argument in a few sentences.

Guidelines

These chapters offer a remarkable insight into some vital things. We are left with a masterclass in understanding the scriptures through God's action in Messiah Jesus and how this can be applied to a concrete situation. And then Paul sums up everything in a beautiful poem giving all the glory to God.

- Are there parallels to the 'weak' and ' strong' in your church communities?
- What can we learn from the way Paul interprets the Hebrew scriptures as 'written for our instruction, so that… we might have hope' (15:4)?
- What might we learn from the way the apostle's carefully laid plans actually turned out?
- Are there things we can learn from Paul about working in teams?
- Why does the letter have so many apparent endings? Do you think the words of 16:25–27 were written by Paul? And are they a fair summary of the message of the letter as a whole? Could you do better?

FURTHER READING

Matthew W. Bates, *Salvation by Allegiance Alone: Rethinking faith, works and the gospel of Jesus the king* (Baker, 2017).

Michael F. Bird, *The Saving Righteousness of God: Studies on Paul, justification and the new perspective* (Paternoster, 2006).

K. P. Donfried (ed.), *The Romans Debate*, revised edition (T&T Clark, 1991).

Paula Gooder, *Phoebe: A story* (Hodder, 2019).

Richard N. Longenecker, *Introducing Romans: Critical issues in Paul's most famous letter* (Eerdmans, 2011).

Richard N. Longenecker, *The Epistle to the Romans (The New International Greek Testament Commentary)* (Eerdmans, 2016).

Peter Oakes, *Reading Romans in Pompeii: Paul's letter at ground level* (SPCK, 2009).

Thomas R. Schreiner, *Romans (Baker Exegetical Commentary on the New Testament)*, second edition (Baker, 2018).

John R.W. Stott, *The Message of Romans* (IVP, 1994).

Anthony C. Thiselton, *Discovering Romans: Content, interpretation, reception* (Eerdmans, 2016).

A.J.M. Wedderburn, *The Reasons for Romans* (T&T Clark, 1991).

N.T. Wright, *Justification: God's plan and Paul's vision* (SPCK, 2009).

The biblical witness to John the Baptist (part I)

David Spriggs

As we prepare to celebrate the first coming of Christ again, an excellent way to do this is to focus on the role of the person whose calling from God was 'to prepare the way of the Lord' (Mark 1:1–4).

'John the baptiser appeared in the wilderness,' Mark tells us, having introduced his gospel with these words: 'The beginning of the good news of Jesus Christ, the Son of God.' Does Mark see John the Baptiser as the opening chapter of the good news, or is he the prequel? Like so much about John, we are immersed straight away into enigmas and questions.

Each of the gospels makes its own contribution to the biblical understanding of John the Baptiser, and across two separate weeks we will be enriched by unravelling much of this complex story. Through this we will be invited to question, to marvel, to worship and to reflect on our mission today.

The present week will look at passages which associate John with the 'coming' of Jesus, mainly as a baby in Bethlehem. The second instalment, in the January 2024 issue of *Guidelines*, will contribute to our Lenten preparations, as much of the later gospel references connect either with Christ's temptations or his redemptive death.

Mark's introduction reminds us that John has a long preparation himself and cannot be understood without engaging with a variety of Old Testament prophetic sayings, which provide a lens for understanding his enigmatic person. But we will also bear in mind that John's impact had a long afterlife too, which is reflected in Acts 19:1–7, and probably in John 3:22–30.

In a parallel way, the gospels indicate that Jesus cannot be understood without receiving the testimony of John to Jesus. To this testimony we now turn, focusing on Luke's contributions.

Unless otherwise stated, Bible quotations are taken from the NRSV.

1 Time to wake up!

Luke 1:5–23

The core of this passage is verse 13: 'Your wife Elizabeth will bear you a son, and you will name him John.' Superficially there is nothing too startling about this, yet almost every word sets us tingling with amazement and anticipation – an appropriate response as we prepare for Advent.

But before we look at the words, we note the speaker – it is an angel, we are first told. Then, moments later, we discover that this is the angel Gabriel himself. The very mention of angels heightens our spiritual alertness, because they indicate that God is significantly moving into action.

This significance is heightened by the venue for this appearance, for it takes place in a very holy place, beside the altar of incense, in the sanctuary of the Lord – a most holy place. Much about this setting would remind alert readers of the angelic visions of the prophet Zechariah, especially the one in chapter 4. Not only the content but also the name of the priest, himself called Zechariah, underline this connection. Here, those famous words addressed to the prophet occur: 'Not by might, nor by power, but by my spirit, says the Lord of hosts,' and, 'Whoever has despised the day of small things shall rejoice' (Zechariah 4:6; 10). This promised son will himself be filled with this Spirit (v. 15) and 'many will rejoice at his birth' (v. 14).

God is on the move! If the context is not enough to alert us, then the content should. At the very founding of Israel, before Israel was Israel, God promised to an elderly couple, well beyond child-bearing aspirations, that he would give them a son. Now Zechariah and his elderly wife are promised the same thing, a son who will be key to the fulfilment of God's promise to bless all the nations of the world (compare Genesis 12:1–2; 15; 17:1–22; 21:1–7).

Like Abraham and Sarah, Zechariah struggles to accept the reality of the promise, even though, like Abraham (see Genesis 15:8), he and Elizabeth his wife are 'righteous before God' (v. 6). But his 'failure' to believe, while it will have detrimental personal consequences, will not frustrate God's purposes of redemption.

What is the role of those who, like us, are standing around and waiting for God's salvation? Luke gives us a clue, 'Now at the time of the incense-offering, the whole assembly of the people was praying outside' (v. 10).

2 Making connections

The birth of a son to an elderly couple is unusual and has covenantal significance. The arrival of the angel Gabriel to announce this conception is also unusual and has covenantal significance. This event is clearly momentous for Elizabeth, Zechariah's wife: 'The Lord has… looked favourably on me and took away the disgrace I have endured among my people' (v. 25). God's intervention is bringing restoration to her standing in the community. Rather than being considered as someone whom God has rejected, she is now in a special place.

We have already been told that Elizabeth's son will have a highly significant ministry, 'to make ready a people prepared for the Lord' by turning many back to the Lord (1:17). But what is the Lord preparing to do?

Enter Gabriel once again, this time to visit a woman, which is rather unusual. As indeed is his message, that she too will conceive even though she isn't yet married. She will be the opposite to Elizabeth; she will now endure disgrace among her people. Indeed, so much disgrace that she leaves her village to be with her elderly relative. Here the two parallel stories begin to knit together as Luke starts to reveal his hand. This elderly relative is none other than Elizabeth, who is now six months pregnant, having herself hidden away for five months.

So Mary 'went with haste' (v. 39). Superficially, this may suggest it was to keep away from any contact with Joseph, to minimise any suggestion of scandal. But at a deeper level it indicates she was acting under divine compulsion (see Luke 2:16).

Twice, Luke links Elizabeth and Mary. First, Elizabeth's pregnancy is an assurance to Mary that Gabriel's words are no empty promise. Already John the Baptist is preparing the way – for Mary to believe. Second, as Mary enters Zechariah and Elizabeth's house , there is a divine witness: 'Elizabeth was filled with the Holy Spirit' (v. 41). She acts as a priestess with her blessing and a prophetess with the recognition of Mary's baby as 'my Lord' (v. 43).

More profoundly, even before his birth, John the Baptist is already witnessing to Jesus: 'The child in my womb leapt for joy' (v. 44). Through John, God is witnessing to the Lordship of Jesus.

3 Time matters

Luke 1:56–66

Often Luke's chronological references are rather vague, such as 'In the days of', 'After those days' or 'In those days'. When he becomes more specific, it is time for us to take note – for instance, the two mentions of 'the eighth day' for the circumcisions of John (v. 59) and Jesus (2:21), thus fulfilling the law's requirements, and the detailed temporal markers for the beginning of the ministry of Jesus, for which John's appearance was the prelude (see 3:1–2). The precise chronology here is intentional – Elizabeth remained in seclusion for five months; Gabriel appeared in the sixth month (that is, of Elizabeth's pregnancy); and Mary remains with her for three months. Luke, as a doctor, is well aware of the period of gestation.

Although commentators understandably conclude that this indicates the likelihood that Mary was present up until the birth of John, we are left unsure here. Maybe her departure is in order to leave the nurture of John to his mother and father. Maybe it is because she was free to return, having seen her elderly relative safely through the last three months of her pregnancy. What it certainly does is shift the focus from John's household back to Mary's story, while underlining the sense that Jesus' life is dependent on John's. Just as his ministry awaits the impact of John's, so his birth awaits John's birth.

The scene which follows Mary's departure relates the naming of 'John' at his circumcision. It is clearly important that his naming is not considered disrespectful to his ancestors, nor arbitrary, nor an indication that he wasn't really born to Zechariah and Elizabeth. It also underlines Zechariah's response of total obedience and trust resulting in the restoration of his ability to speak, 'praising God' (v. 64), preparing for his prophecy in verses 67–79.

Luke's comment that the neighbours and relatives 'were amazed' (v. 63) reflects the sense that this is a divine sign. John has both continuity with the Jewish past, born to righteous parents who are both members of the priestly lineage, and also, with this unexpected name, a break with that past, as the forerunner of the Messiah.

This episode generates a sense of anticipation which draws us in. 'What then will this child become?' He has arrived and become part of the Jewish village community, but this generates more hope: 'For, indeed, the hand of the Lord was with him' (v. 66).

4 Prophetic preparation

In this passage the priest becomes prophet, and yet the prophecy begins with a priestly blessing. Strange things are happening!

Once Zechariah had confirmed his son's name, 'immediately his mouth was opened and his tongue freed, and he began to speak, praising God' (1:64). We should probably understand verses 68 onwards as the first words Zechariah utters. Essentially it is a retrospective view of Israel's salvation history (note the mention of saviour, saved and rescued). There is the affirmation that prophecy had been (or is being) fulfilled, and the confirmation that the covenant with Abraham is being honoured in the present.

Most intriguing is the mention of 'the house of David'. To whom does this refer? It can't be John the Baptist, for he was of priestly descent. It must then mean Jesus. Some think this was an insertion into Zechariah's original words: 'Very probably it was inserted by Luke… with the object once again of toning down the high estimate of John' (Scobie, p. 55). But this is not necessary given the earlier reference to Joseph, 'of the house of David' (1:27), of which Zechariah would be well aware. Verses 68–75 are, then, extolling Jesus, while verses 76–79 relate to John the Baptist.

In these later verses, we see the role of John the Baptist from the inside. He is to be called 'the prophet of the Most High' (v. 76). This picks up on Gabriel's words that John would bring people back to the Lord and himself go before the Lord (1:17). These words could well echo the description of Elijah as serving or standing before the Lord (1 Kings 17:1). It is noticeable that the description of John holding to the Nazirite vows isn't mentioned here, even though the descriptions of him elsewhere echo this.

The core role is that he will prepare the way for the Lord (compare 3:4 but also Mark 1:2–3 (twice), Matthew 3:3 and even John 1:23). Zechariah's prophecy continues with a positive explanatory description, 'to give knowledge of salvation to his people'. As Luke unfolds the story, John sets up the way for salvation to come to Israel, first through the birth of Jesus (2:11, 30) and then through his ministry of repentance for Jesus to commence his ministry (see 3:6; 4:16–30).

5 Still waiting

After his sonorous introduction, Luke has been keeping us waiting! We know, as presumably Theophilus knew (see 'the things about which you have been instructed' – 1:4), that this gospel is really about Jesus, but we have been waiting for the birth of John the Baptist. The events of chapter 1 cover maybe twelve months. Now Luke puts his foot on the accelerator: 'The child grew and became strong in spirit, and he was in the wilderness until the day he appeared publicly to Israel' (v. 80). With this verse approximately 30 years are bridged, in the blink of an eye.

It has often been noted that Luke's birth stories echo others, for example Isaac to Abraham and Sarah, Samuel to Hannah and Elkanah, and Samson to Manoah and his wife. The latter story has a bridging verse too: 'The woman bore a son, and named him Samson. The boy grew, and the Lord blessed him. The spirit of the Lord began to stir him' (Judges 13:24–25). Then, immediately, we are given stories of Samson's exploits to illustrate this 'stirring'. Not with John, however; we will be kept waiting again before his exploits. Jesus takes centre stage – his birth and his childhood being narrated throughout chapter 2. But Luke keeps our attention with the words 'until the day he appeared publicly to Israel' (v. 80).

John is described as being 'in the wilderness' (3:2). Some see in this an indication that John's parents, who were elderly at his birth, had died while he was young and that he was brought up by a religious community like the Essenes or the Qumran Community (see Scobie, pp. 58–59). This is conceivable and might explain where John's ascetic lifestyle, social conscience and even messianic awareness were nurtured. But if so, it wasn't significant for Luke or any other gospel writer to elaborate.

We also recall that another period of waiting for Israel had been 40 years of wandering 'in the wilderness' as the prelude to entering the promised land. These were formative years (as well as being understood as 'punishment' for their disbelief), where Israel received and entered into a covenant with God. It was this covenant that Elijah, mentioned by the angel in 1:17, called Israel to honour as he challenged them to break with their allegiance to Baal worship (see 1 Kings 18:21). Similarly, John called God's people to repent.

6 What to do while waiting?

Luke 3:3–17

Now John's ministry is in full swing. Crowds are coming to him in response to his proclamation of a baptism for repentance. He is fulfilling the prophecy in Isaiah that 'every valley shall be filled… and the rough ways made smooth; and all flesh shall see the salvation of God' (vv. 5–6). He has four related messages for the people, who are understandably 'filled with expectation' (v. 15).

1 Even the demanding ritual of baptism for repentance is not enough on its own. Repentance requires a change of lifestyle.

2 In preparing for the Messiah, relying on Jewish pedigree is futile. God is not dependent on or restricted to national identity. Divine creative power is greater than that and divine judgement is more penetrating than that.

3 Good fruit is required. This will mean different things for different people. The ordinary people must practise justice by sharing their possessions with those who have less. Tax collectors must practise justice by not imposing personal surcharges on other people. Soldiers must practise justice by not misusing their power and position for personal gain.

4 He clearly points away from himself and towards the coming one. He makes it clear that 'the salvation of God' has not yet arrived. At the same time, he heightens the crowd's anticipation of the greatness of this Messiah and the intensity of his mission.

As we move from Advent to Christmas, these are points to bear in mind as we seek to prepare people to encounter the Messiah once again.

1 Coming to church and singing carols is not enough to be ready for God.

2 Claiming our 'Christian birthright' or heritage does not impress God.

3 A serious re-evaluation of our values and actions is called for, so that we are in line with the heart and purposes of God. It is no good simply behaving as our parents or grandparents might have done. We need to understand God's heart for the poor, the vulnerable and the planet.

4 No minister, evangelist or counsellor should be mistaken for the real deal. None of us can in any way replace Jesus. All our ministries and Christmas activities must point away from ourselves and our churches to him.

Guidelines

These early chapters in Luke's gospel associated with John the Baptist focus on three key individuals – Zechariah, Elizabeth and Mary. But most of the time, even if in the background, there are larger groups of people. Their roles provide us with stimulation to consider how we can contribute to the Advent preparation.

- 'Now at the time of the incense-offering, the whole assembly of the people was praying outside' (1:10). Can we encourage our congregations to use Advent as a time for increased prayer, either individually or, even better, together? Is there any better way to prepare for Jesus' birth than spending more time in prayer, thanking God that he fulfils his promises and praying that people will be ready to greet their Saviour?

- 'Meanwhile, the people were waiting for Zechariah, and wondered at his delay in the sanctuary' (1:21). Can we turn the over-busy period of December into a time of excited waiting?

- 'Her neighbours and relatives heard that the Lord had shown his great mercy to her, and they rejoiced with her' (1:58). Can we encourage people to share in the joy that God's coming in Christ can mean for us all? The run-up to Christmas can be so pressurised for families, with extra activities at school and parties to attend. Churches and youth groups can add to the workload, so can we help people by providing space for stress-free times of joy? How can we reduce other activities in the life of our churches so that our leaders can also have time to reconnect with the heart of it and rejoice, rather than arrive at Christmas Eve exhausted?

- 'All these things were talked about throughout the entire hill country of Judea' (1:65). Can we present the 'old story' of Christ's birth in fresh ways that get people talking about 'these things' and lead them to a realisation of the intense wonder at the heart of Christmas?

FURTHER READING

E. Earle Ellis, *The Gospel of Luke (New Century Bible Commentary)* (Marshall, Morgan & Scott, 1981).

I. Howard Marshall, *The Gospel of Luke (New International Greek Testament Commentary)* (Paternoster Press, 1978).

John Nolland, *Luke 1–9:20 (Word Biblical Commentary* (Zondervan, 1989).

Charles Scobie, *John the Baptist* (SCM Press, 1964).

Reading the Bible through the lens of trauma

Karen O'Donnell

When we start to look for them, we quickly realise that the Bible is full of trauma narratives. While medical diagnosis of things such as post-traumatic stress disorder (PTSD) is a relatively modern phenomenon (first occurring in the 1980s), trauma has a long history in human communities. Taking a trauma-informed approach to reading the Bible can sometimes mean identifying narratives where trauma has been glossed over (e.g. the rape of Tamar or the experience of Ezekiel's community), but it can also mean using trauma as a lens to read narratives of remaking and post-trauma flourishing that offer spiritual models of handling trauma to the church today (e.g. Mary's Magnificat or 2 Corinthians). Both approaches are offered in the readings for this week.

Why is it helpful and important to approach reading the Bible with this lens of trauma? It enables honest and rich reflection on texts where difficulties are often glossed over or ignored outright. And it gives voice within such texts to vulnerable, marginalised and ignored people. Allowing these voices to come forth can enable the church to become trauma-informed, to recognise its own complicity in traumatic abuses and to create space in which communities of Christians are able to minister to trauma survivors. Such readings also help to provide language and models of post-traumatic remaking, facilitating the painful process of putting back together in the aftermath of trauma.

These readings come with a warning. Some of them are difficult texts to encounter in a holy book. They can be puzzling, disturbing and challenging. Some readers might find some of the content (violence, rape, suicidal ideation, death) to be triggering. Modes of self-care are always important when encountering such texts. Read with a friend. Read in community. Read when you have time to process your thoughts. Read and be kind to yourself.

Unless otherwise stated, Bible quotations are taken from the NRSV.

1 The rape of Tamar

2 Samuel 13

The rape of Tamar is a disturbing text to find in the Bible, although it is by no means the only account of rape in the Old Testament. This is a text that rarely sees the light of day in our churches – it's certainly not included in the commonly used lectionary, and I can't imagine it's the most obvious choice for a preacher! But this ancient story of rape is a tragically modern one too. The rape of Tamar is one combined with incest and domestic violence. It is set in a conspiracy of men aiding and abetting the crime and a male conspiracy of silence after the fact. Tamar says no, but her no is not respected. Tamar is the only rape victim in scripture to have a voice, but by the end of the story all power to act and speak has been taken away from her. The end of Tamar's story (the eventual murder of the perpetrator Amnon by Tamar's brother Absalom) happens without her.

We find in this narrative an account of a traumatic experience and the demonstration of the symptoms of trauma by the victim Tamar in the aftermath. These symptoms can be characterised by three ruptures. The first is a rupture of the body. Tamar experiences this rupture through the forcible rape by her much stronger brother. Her body is no longer a safe, invulnerable place. The second rupture is one of time. Sexual intercourse, which would usually be reserved for marriage, takes place before such an engagement and Amnon explicitly refuses to marry her when Tamar expresses a legitimate cultural terror of being shamed and cast out as 'damaged goods'. The third rupture is one of language. Tamar does not speak again in the narrative. In fact, Absalom tells her to be quiet. She has no language with which to engage in the meaning making that might enable her future flourishing. She is desolate. The word for 'desolate' – *somema* – is used to refer to a land that is laid waste, referencing Tamar's social abandonment, her psychological state, and, in the ultimate blow to a woman's honour at that time, her childlessness. It is no wonder that this narrative is cited by Phyllis Trible as one of her *Texts of Terror*.

2 The man of sorrows

The book of Lamentations contains five poems expressing intense grief and sorrow in the aftermath of the fall of Jerusalem at the hands of the Babylonian empire in the 6th century BC. In these poems we find two prominent gender-code characters. The first is that of the fallen city – Daughter Zion – who is depicted in Lamentations 1 as a raped and unfaithful wife. The other character is the man of sorrows that we meet in Lamentations 3. In this poem, experiences of trauma are evoked using traditionally masculine tropes of military combat and extreme physical violence. While we might read this poem as an expression of collective trauma after the destruction of Jerusalem, the poem itself is written in the first person, so we might also read it as an account of post-trauma reality.

The man of sorrows is bound in chains; his bones are broken; his skin is wasting away; he is torn to pieces; he is made to cower in the ashes; and he is penetrated with arrows. Who is the perpetrator of this violence towards him? God. In the opening three verses, the man of sorrows makes it clear that his affliction is the result of God's action, of God's wrath. The very being from whom one should expect care and compassion is the one who has turned his hand against him. The man of sorrows experiences such devastating pain that he cannot comprehend how he could rebuild a relationship with God – his abuser (vv. 17–18).

Perhaps, like the rape of Tamar, Lamentations 3 is also an account of rape. It is certainly an account of a loss of masculinity as the man of sorrows becomes prey for the hunter (vv. 10–11) and is pierced by an arrow (v. 12) – a phallic allusion suggesting divine collusion with his rape. His penetrated body puts him in the feminine subject position. His shame and humiliation are palpable (v. 14).

And yet the man of sorrows will not be silenced. He continues to speak and we, the readers, must become witnesses to his trauma – however it is construed. It is through being witnessed and being believed that trauma survivors can begin the process of post-traumatic remaking. Like the man of sorrows, we must call to mind hope – the steadfast love of the Lord never ceases, even though sometimes it feels like it.

3 Disassociation and physic numbing in the exilic community

A reading of the book of Ezekiel is a journey through a strange and violent text, one whose central character – the priest Ezekiel – has been diagnosed with mental illness and possibly even post-traumatic stress disorder (PTSD). While making such a diagnosis through a literary text is dangerous, we can certainly see that this is a text formed in the context of siege warfare and exile. Ezekiel is taken into Babylon in the first wave of exiles and his prophecies offer a meaning-making strategy to the Hebrews that interprets the destruction of Jerusalem and their exile in a way that leaves God in control.

In Ezekiel 24 we find a strange narrative in which God tells Ezekiel that he is going to take away Ezekiel's wife and that Ezekiel is not to mourn her death. That evening Ezekiel's wife dies and the next day Ezekiel does as he is commanded and does not mourn. This is, of course, perplexing to those around him who were well aware of the prescribed customs of mourning. But the point to be made is that God will bring about the destruction of Jerusalem and the exiles should not mourn.

Ezekiel's failure to mourn the death of his wife is a vivid imaging of the psychic numbing experienced by many trauma survivors. Experiencing a kind of 'death in life' is typical for those who experience trauma. In this narrative of an individual's experience, we find a way for the Judean exiles to image their own collective struggle to mourn the destruction of Jerusalem and their exile. Both Ezekiel and the exiles seem to disassociate from their experience. Unable to access this trauma experience directly, the narrative of Ezekiel becomes a place for their collective trauma to be made manifest.

Where does this manifestation of trauma experiences – both individual and collective – lead? The final verse indicates that Ezekiel will eventually find his voice (and perhaps by analogy the exiled Judeans) and no longer be silent. This trauma experience will, eventually, be a sign of God's power: 'They shall know that I am the Lord' (v. 27).

4 The 'unending' gospel

The gospel of Mark is a text that is dominated by Roman trauma. In this, the earliest gospel in the Bible, we find evidence of the early stages of the Jesus movement's grappling with the reality of Jesus' crucifixion, alongside the Roman destruction of Jerusalem and the increasing persecution of Christians. This gospel has been referred to as a passion narrative with a prologue added to it! A full third of the text is given over to Jesus' passion. This passion depicts Jesus as an ambivalent victim of betrayal, trial, flogging and death. Mark's gospel likely preserves an earlier, primitive oral crucifixion narrative.

We see evidence of this early crucifixion narrative and the ways in which Jesus' followers were grappling with the trauma that they had experienced, and which was rooted in the origins of the movement, in the shorter ending of Mark's gospel. You'll notice this in the textual insertion of two sentences between verses 8 and 9. Mark's gospel is a story of the cross without a proper ending. There is no grand resurrection scene but just a group of frightened women running away from the tomb, pledging to say nothing to anyone.

This gospel disappoints our expectation of receiving a conclusive ending to the story. Instead of pulling it all together and wrapping it up, the author of the gospel leaves us peering into the gaping space of an ending that never arrives. How might we resist the urge to wrap this narrative up by supplying the information we have from other gospel accounts? Might there be something useful in this 'unending'?

For many who experience trauma, there is an 'unending' quality to the experience. There is no tidy ending or complete resolution. Rather, there is an ongoing-ness that defies our desires for such resolutions. Mark's unending evokes silence. A literal translation of the Greek would rearrange the words of the final sentence into something like: 'They said nothing to anyone. They were afraid, for…' There is space here for a gesture. A shrug. A silence. In the face of trauma, neat and expected endings are not always possible. Sometimes there is just incomprehension and silence.

5 A letter of trauma recovery

2 Corinthians 1:3–22

While we have only read the very beginning of Paul's second letter to the Corinthians together, it is possible to read the whole of this letter as a kind of memoir of Paul's struggles with traumatic experiences and his strategy of post-traumatic remaking. Here we find a trauma survivor modelling how we might make such a turn towards God in the aftermath of trauma experiences. The first part of our reading (vv. 3–10) is one such account of Paul's experience of affliction. These opening verses attest not to God's rescue of Paul out of trauma but rather Paul's receiving of sustaining courage and grace within such affliction.

Paul tells the Corinthians that he and his companions 'were so utterly, unbearably crushed that we despaired of life itself' (v. 8). This language of desolation (think back to the state of Tamar after she is raped) certainly indicates psychological distress. But these verses also indicate a strategy of trauma survival. Paul is never alone. He connects his own experiences of trauma with the afflictions experienced by the Corinthian community. There is a communion of saints to whom Paul is connected that brings consolation and hope. Throughout this letter, Paul tells and retells stories about his traumatic experiences. This retelling of trauma narratives is an essential part of post-traumatic remaking as each telling provides greater clarity and diminishes the sense of overwhelming such narratives can initially present.

Ultimately, God does not rescue Paul out of trauma, nor does Paul expect God to do so. But in seeking his flourishing both during and after these traumatic experiences, Paul turns to God as 'the Father of mercies and the God of all consolation' (v. 3) to meet him in his affliction. Even in the despairing of life itself, Paul turns to God as the one who raises the dead. The end of this section (vv. 15–22) is a rejection of vacillation and falsehood and an affirmation of truth and the keeping of one's word. Perhaps this emphasis on not letting down the Corinthians is testimony to the source of Paul's own trauma – those who have let him down. In sharp contrast, Paul reminds the Corinthians that in God it is always 'yes'.

6 A song of post-traumatic remaking

We don't tend to think about Mary's experience of the annunciation as a traumatic experience. After all, this event is often played out in the opening scenes of a primary school nativity play, with Mary meekly accepting her fate. And yet the narrative accounts of this event seem to display some trauma symptoms: her bodily integrity is ruptured as her flesh makes way for this unexpected pregnancy; she struggles to make meaning of the experience, asking, 'How can this be, since I am a virgin?' (v. 34); and Mary's sense of time is disrupted as the usual logic of intercourse followed by pregnancy is upended. With these trauma symptoms in mind, we can approach Mary's song of the Magnificat as a narrative of post-traumatic remaking.

Finding a place of safety in her cousin Elizabeth's home, Mary is able to reclaim her bodily integrity and her identity as one who is not a victim. She emerges from this encounter a changed woman. She envisions a new world in which sinful power structures have been overturned. She who was voiceless becomes one who sings out the great redeeming action of God. In the Magnificat, Mary constructs a narrative of her trauma experience that enables meaning-making and flourishing. She identifies herself as one who has received the favour of God, and gives thanks to God as one who is blessed. The second half of the Magnificat takes on the political and juridical flavour of public testimony. Mary reframes her trauma experience as one in which the justice of God is being made known.

In this song, Mary outlines a social action project that will propel her forward into new life. She will make a gift out of the consequences of this trauma (the child Jesus) to the world. Christ in her womb will become a gift of renewal for all people. Mary's reconnection with the world is made complete when she does not stay in her place of safety but rather chooses to return home. Significantly, she is about three months pregnant at this point. Perhaps her morning sickness had died down. Perhaps she was now confident she wouldn't miscarry. It would have been easier for her to stay hidden for the rest of her pregnancy. But Mary chooses to reconnect and bravely faces the world head on.

Guidelines

I wonder how you have found engaging with this lens of trauma in our Bible readings. I suspect it will have been challenging and disturbing even as it may have been hopeful and grace-filled. Giving space to encounter narratives of trauma in the Bible is a risky, but ultimately rewarding, endeavour. On the one hand, we have to wrestle with accounts that seem, like the man of sorrows in Lamentations, to blame God for the traumatic experiences endured. But on the other hand, we encounter songs like the Magnificat in a new light. In engaging in this kind of reading, we are able to witness to trauma and to spiritual modes of remaking in the aftermath of trauma. Death is held in tension with life. Reading the Bible through the lens of trauma disrupts neat binaries of life and death and happy endings. It requires a more nuanced and complex approach to both the text and to reflection on our own experiences.

- What might it mean to resist the urge for a happy ending to difficult experiences? Trauma theologian Shelly Rambo has noted that Christians often want to rush from the crucifixion to the resurrection (i.e. from times of difficulty to the victory of Christ) without attending to the space in the middle. This day is Holy Saturday. It's a day when Jesus is dead and the disciples are hopeless. They do not know the resurrection is coming. What might it mean to give space for Holy Saturday?

- Where is the space for lament and anger in both your own relationship with God and in the church? Before the man of sorrows remembers that God's faithfulness is everlasting, he articulates in detail the devastation he has suffered at the hands of God. He does not attempt to put the blame elsewhere. Is this a helpful way of understanding God's providence? What can you take away from the tension between devastation and God's enduring love that the man of sorrows holds?

- Trauma is an embodied thing. Psychiatrist Bessel van der Kolk tells us that talking therapies will only take us so far in dealing with trauma, but post-traumatic remaking requires the engagement of the body too. What space is there in your own life and ministry for engagement with the body and taking the body seriously as a site of relationship with God? How can your faith become more embodied?

FURTHER READING

Elizabeth Boase and Christopher G. Frechette (eds), *Bible Through the Lens of Trauma (Semeia Studies)* (SBL Press, 2016).

David McLain Carr, *Holy Resilience: The Bible's traumatic origins* (Yale University Press, 2014).

Pamela Cooper-White, *The Cry of Tamar: Violence against women and the church's response* (Fortress Press, 2012).

Serene Jones, *Trauma and Grace: Theology in a ruptured world* (Westminster John Knox Press, 2009).

Bessel van der Kolk, *The Body Keeps the Score: Mind, brain and body in the transformation of trauma* (Penguin, 2015).

Karen O'Donnell, *Broken Bodies: The Eucharist, Mary and the body in trauma theology* (SCM Press, 2018).

Karen O'Donnell and Katie Cross (eds), *Feminist Trauma Theologies: Body, scripture and church in critical perspective* (SCM Press, 2020).

Shelly Rambo, *Resurrecting Wounds: Living in the afterlife of trauma* (Baylor University Press, 2017).

Shelly Rambo, *Spirit and Trauma: A theology of remaining* (Westminster John Knox Press, 2010).

Phyllis Trible, *Texts of Terror: Literary-feminist readings of biblical narratives*, 40th anniversary edition (Fortress Press, 2022).

Advent: the art of waiting

Isabelle Hamley

Every year as I read the Christmas stories, I am struck by the number of characters, and how long in advance these people started moving towards Christmas, without even knowing it. An entire world is moving towards Christmas unawares. In the midst of this lack of awareness, there are some who read the signs, notice glimpses of God at work and hang on to old promises – like the prophets of the Old Testament, or people like Simeon and Anna. Then there are those who are more vaguely aware of the presence of God, but are steeped enough in the stories and teaching that they recognise God at work and respond. They wait and respond in different ways; exploring their words and actions can help us put together a picture of godly and faithful response to promises. But they are not the only ones: there are others, from 'outside', like the magi, whose waiting and response seem tentative and uninformed, yet deeply connected; and those like Herod, who do not want to participate in the promise, but believe enough to feel threatened by it.

These reflections will explore a series of characters: how they are portrayed through scripture; how the patient work of God is gradually revealed; how they make sense of it; and how God evokes different responses. The world of these characters is a world of uncertainty, injustice and violence. They are all positioned differently within it, and with their different socio-economic, religious and political roles come different responsibilities and expectations. Journeying with these people from scripture will help us ask ourselves how we inhabit the promises of God, how we look out for signs of God at work and how we may each be called to respond.

Unless otherwise stated, Bible quotations are taken from the NRSV.

1 The Lord: covenantal waiting

Psalm 103:1–18

'The Lord is merciful and gracious, slow to anger and abounding in steadfast love' (v. 8). This description of God, repeated again and again throughout the Old Testament, provides a bridge and a foundation for thinking about God's action in the incarnation. The God of the Old Testament has an unfair reputation in popular culture, represented as vengeful and angry, impatient with humanity and their sin. This caricature is a far cry from the God of scripture. The God we encounter right from the beginning is the God of this psalm: endlessly patient, a God whose love makes him wait on his creatures patiently, give them chance after chance and only act in anger and punishment when things have become too bad to ignore.

The story of salvation is, at heart, that of the patience of God. In the covenants God makes with his people – Noah, Abraham, Jacob/Israel, Moses, David – God, the God all of things, of time and eternity, the God of holiness and justice, binds himself with limited, frail, stumbling creatures, and promises to walk with them, at a pace that must seem interminably slow. The concept of covenant introduces us to the waiting God, the God of patience and endurance. Israel recognises this and celebrates it repeatedly. This psalm is typical of many biblical songs of praise which recount what God has done and celebrate the fact that God does not respond in judgement to every sin, but makes a generous space for mercy to work in the hearts of human beings.

And yet, as the psalm acknowledges, God does not wait forever: judgement comes, because sin and injustice profoundly disfigure and damage the world and its people. Yet even when God acts in judgement, 'he will not always accuse, nor will he keep his anger forever' (v. 9). Grace and mercy always frame what God does. God's patience is rooted both in God's own nature and character – merciful and gracious, a God of steadfast love – and in God's understanding of humanity: 'he knows how we were made' (v. 14).

As we move into a time of looking ahead towards Christmas, this psalm reminds us of the God who understands everything about humanity and chooses to reveal his glory within it. Furthermore, the whole story reminds us that it is God who waits the longest, as, for centuries and centuries, God walks patiently with his creatures, dealing with their worst while working for the best.

2 Isaiah: prophetic waiting

Isaiah 7:10–16; 9:2–7; 61:1–3

Isaiah is often read in Advent. Some of the prophecies seem to tie closely to the Christmas events, and their poetry and depth speak into today. But the words of Isaiah are often lifted out of their context. The first part of the book of Isaiah (chapters 1—39) is written at a time when Israel is under threat from Assyria. The world is frightening and uncertain before a colonising, brutal superpower. Closer to home, Jerusalem is under attack by its neighbours, Aram and Ephraim. In the midst of this world, Isaiah utters a strange, somewhat discomforting prophecy, of a child whose name, Immanuel, is an assurance of God's presence, who will refuse evil and choose good. But who is this child? And what does God's presence mean? Isaiah offers prophecies that resonate down history. But for the people of Isaiah's time, they must have asked, 'Who? And when?'

When life crowds in and overwhelming political and military forces are at play, what does it mean to hear a promise and live in expectation that God will fulfil it? Even understanding the promise is no easy task. Many expected the child to be a king, a powerful leader who would save Israel and re-establish the nation as an independent and safe entity. They were waiting on God but did not necessarily understand how God would act, and their own fears and hopes shaped the waiting.

Even within the book of Isaiah itself, there are questions about what the promise means. By chapter 40, the people are no longer facing the threat of Assyria; they are in exile, their land taken, their cities ruined, their friends and family dead or forcibly displaced. What do promises and waiting mean when everything seems to say, 'God has forgotten'? This, in many ways, is the heart of much of Isaiah: trying to make sense not just of the waiting, but of what it is people are waiting for. We see inklings in chapters 9 and 61: light and transformation; deliverance from oppression; justice and comfort for the broken and vulnerable. The themes of yesterday's psalm are powerfully echoed: as God comes, the whole of life is transformed and sin is confronted so that justice, peace and mercy can overcome. The question is: is this a comfortable vision? Is it easier to long for justice than actively wait by being transformed in the image of what we know is God's kingdom to come?

3 Simeon and Anna: more prophetic waiting

Luke 2:22–38

Long before the gospel story starts, two people are waiting. Both are prophets. Simeon is waiting for 'the consolation of Israel' and Anna for 'the redemption of Jerusalem' (vv. 25, 38). Both have been waiting their entire lives, steeped in scripture and prayer. Their waiting has been so shaped by the word and presence of God that they immediately recognise that what they have been waiting for is finally here. But I often reflect, in Advent, on their ongoing waiting. Not knowing the shape or time of God's coming, yet unshaken in their life with God. When so many others missed the signs, how did they know? They are not famous, and they do not seem to have much influence. Anna has had a life of sorrow as a childless widow. Yet their lives of patient, faithful waiting were directed towards God.

They do not wait, or respond, in the same way. Both are likely elderly, and both respond faithfully, but with enormous contrast. Simeon utters a song that remains famous, often called the Nunc Dimittis ('Now let [your servant] depart…'). He has waited, and now his work is done. The end of the waiting is the end of his road and he lets go of life, waiting and hoping. He experiences God's faithfulness and is content. Yet his song is followed by a prophecy, ambiguous and ambivalent. He has seen the Messiah, but discerns that the promise does not mean an easy road. The coming of Immanuel will bring challenge and transformation in a world of sin, and even those who think they would welcome the Messiah may find themselves wrong-footed and challenged by the shape of God's coming. Simeon knows that God cannot be contained and is not always welcomed.

Anna's reaction is a complete contrast to Simeon's. She does not move inwards, does not see the fulfilment of the promise as an end for herself, but as a beginning for others. She runs out and tells others about the Messiah and shares the news with 'all who were looking' (i.e. waiting) for the redemption of Jerusalem (v. 38).

Anna and Simeon are both faithful, but they embody different stages of life, despite being equally aged. Simeon speaks of a life well lived and the ability to let go. Anna speaks of discipleship and mission at any age, and of the spontaneous need to share good news. Together, they present a nuanced picture of what is awaited, and how the waiting shapes our responses.

4 Zechariah: no longer waiting

Luke 1:5–25

Before the annunciation, before any sign of the Messiah, two more elderly people are introduced. They are righteous and blameless. They are people of God. It matters that we are told they are righteous, because their inability to have children could have been seen as a curse by onlookers. They are not to blame for their misfortune. The ministry of Jesus will pick up this thread, firmly denying a link between ill health or poverty and sin. To blame others for pain and suffering, to associate these with sin, is to make an argument for the status quo, for maintaining inequality and imbalances of power. The good news of the gospel, as Isaiah prophesied, is one of truth and justice, good news for the poor and oppressed.

We know that Zechariah had prayed for a child – the angel mentions it. But there is no indication of waiting here, unlike with Anna and Simeon. Zechariah is not said to have kept praying. He must have waited, and waited, and waited. He must have read the scriptures and their stories of children in answer to prayer, as with Rachel or Hannah. But this story is closer to that of Abraham and Sarah, though the roles are reversed. Zechariah, just like Sarah, has given up. He is no longer waiting, and the idea that God could still come and bless him and Elizabeth is laughable, illogical, unbelievable.

To wait on God is often to wait against the overwhelming evidence of our senses, reason and the world around us. Waiting is not rational; it is an act of faith. But faith can get tired and weary. Or, for someone hoping for a child, faith can get too painful. For Zechariah, as for Sarah centuries before, to keep hoping against the evidence of time is to keep making yourself vulnerable, fragile and open to disappointment and pain. Anna, who appears later in the gospel, will never have a child. God meets her, but not in answer to this specific longing. There is no controlling the shape of God's promise and revelation.

Zechariah is no longer waiting, so he is surprised by God. He is still said to be faithful and blameless. He had given up on praying for a child, but he had not given up on God. He had just reduced God to human limits and expectations. Ultimately, however, when God appears, Zechariah recognises God, and responds and obeys.

5 Elizabeth: long-suffering waiting

Luke 1:24–25; 39–45; 57–67

Elizabeth is married to Zechariah. Her husband knows something extraordinary is about to happen; he was told Elizabeth would have a child and that this child would be special. But because he was deprived of his voice, he could not explain, could not tell anyone. Elizabeth has no idea, until she herself conceives. We have a little window into Elizabeth's heart. 'For five months she remained in seclusion' (v. 24). Why? After so many years of waiting, was she cautious, in case she lost the child? She cared for herself, minimising risk and exertion. But seclusion may also have cared for her heart, not wanting to expose herself to gossip, unhelpful advice or additional pain should the pregnancy be lost. These first few months of anxious waiting must have stretched out endlessly, mixing joy with anxiety. Elizabeth's waiting is cautious, even in the face of early signs of blessing and the presence of God. Her waiting is shaped, and her hope tempered, by long-suffering.

Elizabeth's reaction contrasts with Zechariah's; she is not disbelieving, but she is anxious. Her faith shines through as she immediately ascribes the pregnancy to God's action: 'This is what the Lord has done for me.' Yet she also alludes to her pain: 'the disgrace I have endured' (v. 25). She is said to be blameless and righteous, but in her own eyes she is disgraced and bears the weight of others' judgement. By granting her a child, God is already fulfilling the promise to lift up those who are oppressed or vulnerable.

Elizabeth and Zechariah are linked to priestly families and held in high regard, especially following the birth of this special child, announced by angels. Their status is not that of kings, but it will be enough to provide a safe refuge for Mary, the pregnant teenager, as they choose to use their position for the sake of others. Their respectability offers her a shelter and they recognise that she, too, is carrying a special child.

Elizabeth and Zechariah are shaped by the stories of scripture and a life of prayer, so that they recognise God at work, not only in their own life but also in the lives of others. And Zechariah brings his knowledge of scripture and his recognition of God at work far beyond his own life, and crafts a hymn which Christians the world over still know and sing, the Benedictus, a psalm of praise for the God coming to save.

6 Mary: waiting for transformation

Luke 1:26–56

Mary's story is often told as a 'beginning', though she only arrives a very long way into the story, centuries and even millennia into the waiting. Like Elizabeth, Zechariah, Simeon and Anna, Mary is not a big player in the official histories of her world. She is not even a bit player. She is small, unknown, disregarded. She comes into the story as a young woman whose life ahead had been planned with simple, normal expectations.

And yet… Mary surprises us and shows that her life has been shaped by the stories and teachings of those who have been waiting for God for many years. First, she correctly realises that an angelic visitation is strange and not necessarily a sign of good fortune. The greeting, 'favoured one', is one that suggests there is some special task ahead. Mary is 'perplexed', presumably both because of her perception of herself as of little significance and because the requests of the Lord rarely lead you on an easy path. But Mary agrees, and immediately seeks the counsel of those she knows to be wise and in tune with God, which shows her own wisdom: knowing when she needs help, knowing her limits and trying to make sense of God's actions within the community of faith, rather than independently. To discern God at work is something the people of God do together.

We really come to understand Mary with her song of verses 46–55, the Magnificat. It is presented here as a spontaneous song, but it is steeped in the words and forms of Israel's scriptures. It is a psalm extolling the actions of God and God's transformation of the world, with a particular focus on justice. Mary is in tune with the Psalms, with Isaiah and with the prophets in the themes she highlights: God is saviour; God chooses to work through the small and lowly; God is mighty and holy; God extends mercy for generations; God ushers in an upside-down kingdom within which normal social expectations of status, power and wealth are overturned; and God fulfils God's promises. Mary knew the scriptures and had taken on the prophets' waiting as her own. Here, in the Magnificat, she proclaims not just what God is about to do, but what God has already done. God's action in Jesus reflects God's actions throughout history. The kingdom has been coming in glimpses already, for those with the eyes to see it.

Guidelines

A broad look at scripture shows God's action throughout the centuries, revealing God's patience and planning. Throughout, justice and righteousness are identified as integral to salvation. In the waiting of prophets and of the people of the gospel, God's promise was about the transformation of the whole of society and relationships between people, not just the transformation of individual hearts.

- How does the emphasis on justice in Isaiah and other prophets help us understand the ministry of Jesus and the shape of our own discipleship?
- We meet people, throughout the story, with different reactions to waiting, promise and fulfilment. Who do you identify with the most? Why might that be?
- Zechariah stands out as a man of God, who has nonetheless come to a place of cynicism and tiredness. Do you know anyone like this? How do you deal with these feelings within yourself, or help others struggling with them?
- Simeon and Anna embody very different reactions to the coming of Jesus. One, Simeon, recognises that his task and waiting are done, while the other, Anna, embraces a new calling, moving out of the temple and among the people to proclaim the good news. How might you help those who need to lay down ministries and callings? And how might you nurture the calling of all, regardless of age or stage of life?
- It is striking that the response of each character is shaped by knowledge and understanding of scripture and a practice of prayer. What habits do you nurture within your own life to help you discern God at work and shape your own expectations of how God may act?

1 Joseph: a prism for humanity

Matthew 1

The gospel of Matthew, opening the New Testament, defies modern literary conventions. Unlike Hollywood films or contemporary novels, it doesn't start with exciting events, a mystery or a cliffhanger. It starts with the genealogy of Jesus, an account of people who gave birth to other people. It may sound dull today, but to an ancient reader well versed in scripture, it would have sounded intriguing. Abraham, David and the Messiah in one sentence, right at the start, promises great things, an exciting story. The very word 'Messiah' suggests that what Israel has been awaiting for so long has finally come!

And yet – the Messiah's genealogy includes plenty of unknown people, including his father, Joseph. This in itself undermines expectations and creates a degree of mystery: why would the Messiah come to a man so unremarkable? On the other hand, Joseph can trace his lineage back to David, which fulfils the promise of a messiah from the house of David. As always, it is the detail that is fascinating and gives us clues to the importance of the genealogy.

Unusually, four women appear: Tamar, Rahab, Ruth and Bathsheba. That the Messiah should be descended from these four women creates all the mystery and surprise that the beginning of a story could possibly want. Tamar was a neglected widow, unfairly treated, who tricked her father-in-law into sleeping with her so that she would conceive a son. Rahab was a Canaanite, a prostitute from Jericho who avoided being put to death because she extended kindness to Hebrew spies and confessed belief in God. Ruth was a Moabite, one of the most hated of Israel's neighbours, whom they were forbidden to marry; yet she married an Israelite man, was widowed and then decided to remain faithful to Israel, its people and their God. Bathsheba, finally, was the woman who King David tore away from her husband to satisfy his lust – a story of sexual violence and murder.

Right here, in the genealogy of Jesus through Joseph, are encompassed the tears and triumphs of humanity. Sin and brokenness are deeply etched within it, yet so are faith and faithfulness. The genealogy proclaims a Messiah who comes for the sinful and the broken, for Israel and Gentiles alike, and who confounds the expectations of those waiting by embracing, rather than judging, his people's frail humanity.

2 Patient waiting

Curiously, in all the narratives of the lead-up to Christmas, one person is often forgotten: the foetus developing slowly in Mary's womb, barely noticeable for several months. This growing child is none other than the God of the entire universe.

As we start moving towards Christmas, it is worth pausing and reminding ourselves of who this God is: the God of Genesis, the God who creates everything. The God who created the earth and all the stars, galaxies and far-flung worlds we are barely aware of. The God who created the immense abundance and complexity of all life on earth. This God, who holds immensity and eternity in his hand, is now held within one single cell, then two, then four, and so on.

What would waiting in the womb for nine whole months, constrained and cooped up, have been like? What would this immense intelligence and compassion have felt like, reduced to so little and incapable of much movement, or of influencing the world around? How could this be a step forward, to something better? To be an embryo, then a foetus, is to be utterly dependent and vulnerable to the world around. And the world around Mary was in many ways a harsh world: a world of Roman oppression, of poverty and of poor health outcomes for many women and their babies. For the God who had been patiently waiting on humanity and working with them through the covenant, this manner of coming was a huge risk – and an extraordinary statement.

These nine months of waiting, and a childhood of growing, show a God willing to enter into his creatures' reality and to wait in the way they have been waiting for him to act, experiencing the same constraints, fears and dangers.

God here is affirming the human body; God is affirming what is small, what is invisible or what is barely noticeable. God is affirming the vulnerable and dependent, and proclaims that true power does not lie primarily or solely in dazzling acts of independent strength, but in how this power is used, controlled and moderated in the service of all. God challenges all the powers of the world, all the wisdom and knowledge of the world, and reorders expectations and values by embodying, in the most human way possible, a different way of being.

3 John the Baptist: proactive waiting

Luke 1:41; 3:1–18; 7:18–23

John the Baptist is poised between waiting and responding. His first appearance is a spontaneous response to the presence of God – leaping in the womb, heightening his mother's consciousness of God, and Elizabeth is filled with the Spirit. Right from the start, John points away from himself and brings others closer to God. This will be the sign of his ministry throughout: preparing the way, preparing others for the coming of God.

Jesus has not come into the fullness of his ministry as John starts out on his; therefore John is caught in the reality that God has already come, is already doing something new, but is not yet revealed fully. It is not clear yet who Jesus exactly is or what Jesus will do. John himself will send out messengers to ask Jesus whether he is 'the one who is to come' (7:20). John has been waiting for the Messiah, walking closely with God and reading the signs of God at work. But that does not mean everything is clear; John still struggles with a degree of doubt about his hopes, and the length and outcome of his waiting. Jesus' words in answer point, not to himself, but back to Isaiah, and encourage John to trust his reading of scripture to help him know God.

Questions, however, do not mean that John is inactive or paralysed. John has learnt, from the scriptures, the prophets, his parents and a life of prayer and seeking God, that whatever stage of waiting we may be at, some things are certain: the call to holiness, to justice, to righteousness, to repentance and to a close walk with God. John does not simply seek these things for himself, but, just like the long line of Israel's prophets, he calls others to turn towards God. His waiting is not alone in a temple, or alone in a desert. It is proactive waiting that seeks to see the promised kingdom of the future transform the present.

Ultimately, this is the key to waiting: one cannot hope for a different future without that hope shaping our actions, beliefs and choices for today. When we pray, 'Your kingdom come,' we not only express a wish for tomorrow, but also make a statement about the shape of life we believe is right, good and holy. John is inviting all those listening to him not to wait for God's extraordinary action tomorrow, but to respond to God's existing invitation to walk with him today.

4 The magi: the waiting of watchers

We usually meet the magi, or kings, at Christmas only, coming to meet the Christ-child after the birth. Their journey, however, would have started many months before, their waiting even longer ago. Unlike Mary, John, Zechariah, Elizabeth, Simeon and Anna, they do not seem to have Israel's scriptures to guide them. They come 'from the East' (v. 1); they do not belong to the long line of people who have received the promise and waited throughout history. They are counterparts to Ruth and Rahab in Jesus' genealogy. They are Gentiles who seek God, to whom God reveals himself.

This pattern is not new in scripture. Even though the Old Testament concentrates on the story of God's covenant with Israel, others regularly appear in the narratives, outsiders who have heard of God, know God and have something to share about God with the people of the promise. Melchizedek, whose name means 'king of righteousness', feeds and blesses Abraham (Genesis 14:18–20). Jethro, Moses' father-in-law, helps Moses learn the craft of good leadership (Exodus 18); Rahab shelters Israelites in Canaan (Joshua 2:1–7); Ruth the Moabite cares for her mother-in-law and marries into Israel (Ruth 1—4). In all these stories, God is at work outside of Israel.

God's promise is for a Messiah, for redemption, for transformation. But God is not idle in the waiting, and God does not concentrate his love and action on one people to the exclusion of all others. God moves in the wider world and responds to those who seek him. The foreign magi have followed a star, an unusual event interpreted correctly. At the same time, they show a lack of familiarity with the ways of God. They look for a king in a palace, among oppressors, in wealth and opulence first; the history of Israel suggests that God consistently chooses the unexpected as leaders and overturns expectations.

Yet they are not fazed by their mistake, and quietly accept the king born in a stable as they follow the star; God then clearly speaks to them with a warning in a dream: they may not know all the stories, they may not be shaped by prophets and promise, but they are open enough to God to hear God's voice and follow God's path. They, like John the Baptist and others, practise an active waiting, seeking God, looking out for signs of God's presence, and go out of their way to be where God is at work.

5 Herod: fear and expectations of challenge

Herod is a villain, though we rarely attend to the extent of his evil – or its roots. Herod is waiting and expecting, too. He is not, however, expecting good things or waiting for God to act. He is living in fear of God and the people acting in response to the injustice and inequality that he represents. For those who rule by fear and brutality, the people are always a threat, and no time is ever safe.

If we read the story of Herod against the background of the prophecies and psalms uttered by others, he has good reason to fear. Mary's song, the Magnificat, is a direct challenge to his position in life: '[God] has scattered the proud in the thoughts of their hearts. He has brought down the powerful from their thrones, and lifted up the lowly; he has filled the hungry with good things, and sent the rich away empty' (Luke 1:51–53). The writings of all the prophets of Israel speak of a time of God's action, bringing a king of justice and righteousness. Herod may not know the God of Israel, but he no doubt knows of the things Israel believes; and even if he does not know Israel's scripture, he will know, from the history of humanity, that tyrants and occupiers are always more vulnerable than they like to portray. The birth of a possible king has kindled hope, and hope is a threat – it lifts those who are oppressed and gives them something to live and fight for.

Herod is not unique; he is not an example of unprecedented evil. His story parallels that of another fearful tyrant, Pharaoh. Pharaoh was afraid of Israel and tried to quell the people's hopes through redoubled oppression. Pharaoh also ordered the widespread massacre of small children. Both men show the length to which a threatened leader may go to keep hold of power. Both display the results of living with both the expectation that others may rise up and the hope that they themselves would remain safe. What shapes their waiting is self-interest and belief in their own power over the course of history. God, meanwhile, is at work among those who know they have little power, but believe in the one who does.

6 The waiting of heaven

Luke 2:1–18; 1 Peter 1:10–12

Angels appear repeatedly in the Christmas narratives: to Zechariah, Mary, Joseph and the shepherds. Yet we rarely credit them as characters in their fullness, maybe because we know very little about them. Angels appear regularly in scripture and are a common feature of the Old Testament. In both Greek and Hebrew, the word 'angel' means messenger, someone sent by God for a clear purpose, with a specific message or task. At the beginning of the gospels, angels come with good news, announcing an end to waiting and the beginning of the fulfilment of the promise. Only moments later, an angel warns Joseph of the danger Herod presents and propels the little family into exile in Egypt. In the Old Testament, angels regularly bring warnings and calls to repentance. They can also bring judgement and destruction, as in Sodom and Gomorrah (Genesis 19). The angels of scripture are not the fluffy, benign figures of popular imagination. They can be fearsome and do not bend to human designs: they are messengers of God himself and will only partake in the purposes of God.

The presence of angels alerts us to a reality far beyond our own; just as God himself has been waiting, working and moving towards the renewal of all things, the whole of heaven has been too. God's work of salvation is all-encompassing and calls all to join in. It operates on a cosmic scale and involves the waiting of heaven for far longer than humans remember waiting on God.

And at Christmas, at the moment of incarnation, something extraordinary happens. Something that the host of heaven, however involved they have been in working alongside God, somehow do not quite share, or know, or grasp. The epistle of Peter puts it this way: that the good news of the gospel, of God made human, of salvation, is something 'into which angels long to look' (1 Peter 1:12). Angels here are spectators, facilitators. But God becomes human. It is completely inhabiting the limitation and frailty of humanity that changes the course of history. How easily do we forget quite how extraordinary this move is? Peter reminds us of the strangeness and unexpectedness of Christmas. What God actually did was beyond what earth and heaven could comprehend. All space and time were concentrated in this one small, squalling human. All power was reduced to a dependent little child, all rules and expectations upturned and confounded, so that all could be made new.

Guidelines

It is easy to domesticate Christmas, to think of cuddly babies, fluffy donkeys and beautiful angels. The story we have, however, is far grimmer, and far more challenging. It is a story of radical justice and challenge to all the ways of earth and the way in which the people of earth use and misuse power. It is a profound challenge to how human beings think it is possible to influence the world around them and change the course of history. It is an inescapable call to re-interpret how we are meant to inhabit the world, as interdependent, fragile creatures, who nonetheless have moral choices and agency, whatever our circumstances may be.

- Christmas is a story of prejudice, injustice and inequality. It is a story of political oppression, wanton murder and forced displacement. It is a story that begs us to ask, how do we relate to political leaders? How do we react to injustice and to those who are maimed, displaced and dispossessed?

- What do we expect God to do in bringing about his kingdom of peace and justice, and how does this change the way in which we live today?

- What stories and habits help us become people who live the life of the kingdom to come in the reality of today?

- Maybe this Christmas, you could spend time praying the prayers of the people who waited in scripture: Isaiah, Zechariah, Simeon, Mary. How do these prayers sound in the light of current events around the world? What might active waiting for these prayers to be answered look like for you?

FURTHER READING

Brevard S. Childs, *Isaiah: A commentary (Old Testament Library Series)* (Westminster John Knox, 2000).

Luke T. Johnson, *Sacra Pagina: The gospel of Luke* (The Liturgical Press, 1991).

Donald Senior, *Matthew (Abingdon New Testament Commentaries)* (Abingdon Press, 1998).

John 15: abide and go

Leoné Martin

John 15 is all about relationships. The rich imagery of the vine and the branches, sandwiched between two discourses about the work of the Holy Spirit, depicts not only the relationship between the Godhead and disciples but also the relationship between spiritual formation and mission. Containing the last of seven 'I am' statements in the gospel of John, it continues to shed light on Jesus' contested identity. Through these statements, Jesus declares and affirms who he is above the voices of challenge, accusation and questioning. It is through Jesus' self-declaration of who he is and what he has been sent to do that the disciples begin to develop a sense of their identity and mission in relationship to him.

These passages are significant, forming part of Jesus' final words before he completes his journey to the cross. His time was running out, so he had to be selective about what he said (John 16:4–5, 12). He wanted his disciples to understand how to remain in a life-giving relationship with him once he was no longer with them in bodily form. He was equipping them to continue his work and mission in the world.

Often there is a temptation to pit the practice of spiritual disciplines against participation in evangelism and social action, as though deep spirituality is at odds with exercising human agency and taking action. However, John 15 illuminates how intimacy with God and action in the world are tightly woven together, creating a tapestry that only makes sense with the presence of both strands. Over the next week, we will explore how our participation in the mission of Jesus flows out of our life-giving relationship with him.

Unless otherwise stated, Bible quotations are taken from the NRSV.

1 Intimacy produces fruitfulness

John 15:1–5

Repeatedly in the Old Testament, vine imagery is used in reference to Israel. However, God often judges Israel for being a vine that does not produce good fruit (e.g. Isaiah 5:1–7). In contrast to Israel, Jesus asserts himself as the 'true vine', because where Israel failed to fulfil the will of God, he succeeded.

The vine imagery is also used to describe the interconnected relationship between Jesus and the Father, and the Godhead and the believer. The Father is described as the 'vine-grower' or, understood in another way, the gardener – the one who nurtures and tends to the vine to promote growth and flourishing. The disciples of Jesus, on the other hand, are likened to the branches in the vine. It is the Father's role to remove unfruitful branches so they don't hinder the flourishing of the vine and to prune the fruitful branches so they can produce even more abundantly.

The use of the word 'prune' is a play on words, as the Greek root for the words 'prune' and 'cleanse' is the same. This reference to cleansing acts as a bridge between this discourse and the prophetic act of Jesus washing the disciples' feet recorded in John 13. The point is that neither salvation nor sanctification are things the disciples can do for themselves. God takes the initiative.

The fruitfulness of the branches depends entirely on the nurture of the vine-grower and their proximity to the vine. Often our culture prizes feverish activity, linking this with productivity. These verses challenge the understanding that fruitfulness comes from striving, because the fruitfulness God desires for us comes from abiding in Christ. It's our vital union and proximity to Christ that enables us to produce. Fruitfulness, according to John 15:4–5, is a product of intimacy with God.

The Greek word *menó*, translated as 'abide', means to remain, stay and dwell. The invitation to abide in Jesus is connected to the promise that Jesus will abide in us. Through this two-way abiding, disciples can bear not only some fruit but 'much fruit'. Abiding is about drawing close to Jesus; it is the distant, unconnected believer who becomes unproductive.

2 Abiding

Intimacy with Christ is not merely about productivity but crucially about spiritual vitality and life. Branches not connected to Christ the vine have nothing to sustain them and die. While the symbolic language of being 'thrown into the fire, and burned' (v. 6) may conjure up ideas of God's judgement and hell, I believe this would be to stretch the analogy too far. Instead, it highlights the consequence of disconnection: branches that do not remain in the vine become unproductive and useless.

Jesus unpacks further what it means to abide and the benefits to the believer. Fruitfulness is also experienced in the joy of answered prayer. The bold assertion, 'Ask for whatever you wish, and it will be done for you' (v. 7), is made based on the word of Jesus abiding in the one who is asking. When the word of Christ abides in the one who is asking, they will not ask amiss, but rather what they request in prayer will be in alignment with the will of God.

To abide in Jesus is also to abide in his love. The love Jesus shows and demonstrates to believers flows from the love and relationship Jesus has with the Father. The relationship between the persons of the Trinity – Father, Son and Holy Spirit – is one of love. The disciples are caught up in the love that flows through and out of the Godhead. Jesus loves his disciples the same way the Father has loved him. On this basis, he implores the disciples to follow his example as he has followed the Father's.

Love, according to verse 10, is not a feeling but acting in obedience. It is by heeding Jesus' commands that believers remain in his love. Again we are to do as Jesus does, as his obedience to the Father is how he abides in his love. This command is not to suggest that we can earn the love of God, but rather obedience should flow out of the love we have for Jesus; it is a demonstration of our love. Disciples, by their very nature, follow and learn from their teacher. It is by following Jesus' example of abiding in the love of God and following the commands of God that the disciple bears fruit and the Father is glorified.

3 Friends of Jesus

Joy and friendship are the fruit of obedience. Since obedience is crucial to producing this fruit, Jesus delves deeper into what he is commanding and how obedience should be demonstrated. His command is for the disciples to love each other as he has loved them (v. 12). This statement provides the key to understanding what it means to abide in the love of Christ. To abide in Jesus' love is to demonstrate the same level of sacrificial love to other disciples that he has shown to us.

In describing the sacrificial love he was commanding, Jesus points towards his looming crucifixion and death. He is preparing to show them and us the ultimate demonstration of his love through the laying down of his life. To imitate him, his followers also need to lay down their lives for each other and, in doing so, his followers will become his friends.

Obedience leads to this change in the nature of the relationship between Jesus and his followers. Ironically, obeying your master's commands would be more easily associated with servitude than friendship. The distinction is linked to revelation; servants do what their master says without insight into their master's plans or purposes. Conversely, friends are privy to inside information; with friends we share our most intimate secrets and plans. In the context of his friendship with the disciples, Jesus has revealed 'everything' that he has heard from his Father. This level of transparency is astonishing. Jesus has held nothing back from his disciples, although it is clear at times they may not fully understand what is being revealed to them (e.g. John 14:5).

Friendship with Jesus is closely connected to receiving his joy. Often obedience is associated with thankless and robotic drudgery. However, obeying Jesus' command to love is connected to a sense of well-being, pleasure and joy. It's important to realise the joy that Jesus promises is not the absence of persecution or trouble but peace in the midst of it and hope in a world tainted by a sense of hopelessness. As we will explore later this week, friendship with Jesus often means enmity with the world.

4 Go

John 15:16–17

Throughout John 15, fruitfulness is linked to remaining. However, verse 16 makes clear that remaining is not about being static. On the contrary, the disciples are commanded to 'go' and bear fruit. The Greek word *hupago* means to literally go away or depart. The inclusion of the word 'go' is intentional, signifying the disciples being sent out on a fruit-bearing mission in the world. A branch cannot eat its own fruit; in the same way, the fruit that the disciples produce is not for their consumption but for the benefit of others.

Fruitfulness is closely linked to the command to love and to replicate the sacrificial love of Christ. However, it could also be understood as the disciples' calling to self-replicate and make more disciples. One of the main characteristics of fruit is that it has the potential to reproduce itself according to its kind. Therefore, the fruitfulness of the disciples can be understood as reproducing Jesus' character and his good works, including making new disciples.

Yet the initiative in this endeavour is not taken by the disciples but by Jesus. It is Jesus who has chosen and appointed them to be fruitful. The term 'appoint' suggests that Jesus has chosen them with a specific job in mind. The disciples are chosen for the participation in and continuation of Christ's mission. In the same way that the Father sent Jesus, the disciples are sent by the Son into the world to bear good fruit.

The imagery of the vine and the branches brings to life how inseparable the mission of the disciples is from the mission of Jesus. Together they are one fruit-bearing organism. The disciples are utterly dependent on Jesus for success, with Jesus selecting and setting them apart. Remaining, then, is not a physical location but a spiritual reality. The disciples need to remain in Jesus even as they go out to participate in his mission in the world.

Interestingly, the fruit the disciples are chosen and appointed to bear is fruit that will 'abide'. Although the word is translated as 'fruit that will last' in the NRSV, it is the same Greek word *menó* used repeatedly in John 15 to describe the branches' relationship to the vine. Disciples that abide are enabled to produce abiding fruit.

5 The cost of relationship

While friendship with Jesus is associated with numerous benefits, it is not without its costs. Persecution is no surprise to Jesus (v. 25), but he is keen that it will also be no surprise to his followers. Their intimacy with him will attract hatred from the world, and he takes time to warn them of this reality.

To be chosen by Jesus means to be rejected by the world. Before being chosen and entering into a relationship with Jesus, they belonged to the world, sharing the same values and practices. However, as soon as they are chosen out of the world, they became at odds with its value system.

Hatred for Jesus is synonymous with hatred for the Father because of the inseparable nature of their person. In the same way, the dual abiding of Jesus dwelling in his disciples and his disciples dwelling in him means that they not only share in his mission but also in his persecution. As servants sent to carry out his mission in the world, they can expect to receive the same treatment as the one they are representing.

It is their persecutors' lack of relationship with the Father that results in the hatred that Jesus and his followers will endure. Their persecutors may know the Father by name, but they lack the intimacy of relationship to know him by nature. However, not knowing the Father does not absolve them from the guilt of rejecting Jesus. Witnessing the words and works of Jesus leaves them without a valid excuse for their ignorance. Their ignorance is a choice rooted in their desire to protect and preserve their power. They have no valid justification for hating Jesus, since his works are good and authenticate his identity as the Son of God.

Being chosen to bear fruit also means being chosen to bear persecution. The disciples will imitate Jesus by producing fruit in the presence of persecution. Like Jesus, their good words and works will not always be welcomed or celebrated. While intimacy with Jesus attracts the cost of persecution, the same intimacy enables the disciples to bear the cost. Their consolation will come from remembering that they are suffering in the name of Christ.

6 Joining the Spirit in the mission of God

John 15:26–27

The disciples may find themselves hated by the world, but they will not be alone. Jesus promises to send the *paraklétos*, translated as an 'advocate'. However, the word has a broader range of meanings, including helper, assistant and comforter. The disciples are chosen to be representatives of Jesus continuing his mission, but the Holy Spirit will power the mission. The Holy Spirit will provide the comfort they need to endure persecution and the help they need to testify to who Jesus is.

In the same way that Jesus came from the Father, the Spirit too is sent by Jesus from the Father. This sending sequence signifies a continuation of God's mission to redeem and restore creation. When Jesus ascends to heaven, he sends the Holy Spirit into the world to empower generations of disciples to continue his mission of self-replication.

The Holy Spirit is sent not only to help the disciples but also to testify on Jesus' behalf. It is through the Spirit that the truth about who Jesus is and what he has done can be known. By joining the Spirit in testifying about Jesus, the disciples become part of making more disciples who follow and obey Jesus' teachings. Importantly this is not human-initiated but Spirit-initiated. The disciples are invited to join in with the work of the Spirit in the world.

The disciples are able to testify because they have been with Jesus 'from the beginning' (v. 27). It is their relationship with Jesus that makes testifying possible. Had they not had an intimate relationship with Jesus where they were able to witness his works and character, they would have nothing to share with others. They would not be able to give evidence about his person and power. It is the same for the church today: we are only able to testify accurately about Jesus to the degree that we know him. That is why our proximity to Jesus and our friendship with him are so crucial to our ability to participate in the mission he has sent us on. Fruitful mission is a joint venture; we can't do it without Jesus and Jesus chooses not to do it without us. We are chosen and empowered to participate.

Guidelines

Alan Donaldson, general secretary of the European Baptist Federation, beautifully captured the relationship between abiding and going in a demonstration he shared during a sermon. He invited his wife to join him on stage and they began to dance. They started close, then he spun her outward away from his body, constantly connected, hand in hand, before whirling her back in to his embrace. This demonstration brought to life the delicate dance we are called to participate in with the Holy Spirit, characterised by times of private intimacy and public activism, and all the while constantly connected to Christ. The command to go and bear fruit does not nullify the call to abide. Even as disciples venture out to bear fruit, we are to remain in life-giving union with the vine. It is our vital union with Jesus that makes the mission possible, in terms of both multiplication and acts of compassion. Intimacy and action are not opposed, but rather work hand in hand.

- How do you understand Jesus' invitation for you to abide in him? Has your understanding of what it means to abide changed? If so, how?
- What does fruitfulness look like for you?
- What does it mean to you to be a friend of God? What are some of the benefits and costs of this special relationship?
- How have you suffered because of your relationship with Christ? How does John 15:18–25 help you to understand that suffering?
- Where do you sense the Spirit calling you to join in with Jesus' mission in the world?
- How would you describe the relationship between spiritual intimacy and mission? Has your understanding of this relationship changed? How?

FURTHER READING

George Beasley-Murray, *John (Word Biblical Commentary)* (Zondervan Academic, 2018).

Mae Elise Cannon, *Just Spirituality: How faith practices fuel social action* (InterVarsity Press, 2013).

Tony Evans, *The Tony Evans Bible Commentary: Advancing God's Kingdom Agenda* (Broadman & Holman Publishers, 2019).

Jey J. Kanagaraj, *John (New Covenant Commentary)* (Wipf and Stock Publishers, 2013).

Become a Friend of BRF
and give regularly to support our ministry

We help people of all ages to grow in faith

We encourage and support individual Christians and churches as they serve and resource the changing spiritual needs of communities today.

 | Through **Anna Chaplaincy** we're enabling churches to provide spiritual care to older people

 | Through **Living Faith** we're nurturing faith and resourcing life-long discipleship

 | Through **Messy Church** we're helping churches to reach out to families

 | Through **Parenting for Faith** we're supporting parents as they raise their children in the Christian faith

Our ministry is only possible because of the generous support of individuals, churches, trusts and gifts in wills.

As we look to the future and make plans, **regular donations make a huge difference** in ensuring we can both start and finish projects well.

By becoming a Friend of BRF and giving regularly to our ministry you are partnering with us in the gospel and helping change lives.

How your gift makes a difference

£2 a month — Helps us to give away **Living Faith** resources via food banks and chaplaincy services

£10 a month — Helps us to support parents and churches running the **Parenting for Faith** course

£5 a month — Helps us to support **Messy Church** volunteers and grow the wider network

£20 a month — Helps us to develop the reach of **Anna Chaplaincy** and improve spiritual care for older people

How to become a Friend of BRF

Online – set up a Direct Debit donation at brf.org.uk/donate or find out how to set up a Standing Order at brf.org.uk/friends

By post – complete and return the tear-off form opposite to 'Freepost BRF' (*no other address or stamp is needed*)

If you have any questions, or if you want to change your regular donation or stop giving in the future, do get in touch.

Contact the fundraising team

Email: giving@brf.org.uk
Tel: 01235 462305
Post: Fundraising team, BRF, 15 The Chambers,
               Vineyard, Abingdon OX14 3FE

Registered with
FUNDRAISING
REGULATOR

Bible Reading Fellowship (BRF) is a charity (233280) and company limited by guarantee (301324),
registered in England and Wales

GL0323

SHARING OUR VISION – MAKING A GIFT

I would like to make a donation to support BRF.
Please use my gift for:

☐ Where it is most needed   ☐ Anna Chaplaincy   ☐ Living Faith
☐ Messy Church   ☐ Parenting for Faith

Title	First name/initials	Surname
Address		
		Postcode
Email		
Telephone		
Signature		Date

Our ministry is only possible because of the generous support of individuals, churches, trusts and gifts in wills.

Please treat as Gift Aid donations all qualifying gifts of money made (*tick all that apply*)   *giftaid it*

☐ today,   ☐ in the past four years,   ☐ and in the future.

I am a UK taxpayer and understand that if I pay less Income Tax and/or Capital Gains Tax in the current tax year than the amount of Gift Aid claimed on all my donations, it is my responsibility to pay any difference.

☐ My donation does not qualify for Gift Aid.

Please notify BRF if you want to cancel this Gift Aid declaration, change your name or home address, or no longer pay sufficient tax on your income and/or capital gains.

You can also give online at **brf.org.uk/donate**, which reduces our administration costs, making your donation go further.

Please complete other side of form ➲

SHARING OUR VISION – MAKING A GIFT

Please accept my gift of:

☐ £2 ☐ £5 ☐ £10 ☐ £20 Other £ [   ]

by (*delete as appropriate*):

☐ Cheque/Charity Voucher payable to 'BRF'

☐ MasterCard/Visa/Debit card/Charity card

Name on card

Card no. [ ][ ][ ][ ] [ ][ ][ ][ ] [ ][ ][ ][ ] [ ][ ][ ][ ]

Expires end [M][M] [Y][Y]   Security code* [ ][ ][ ]   *Last 3 digits on the reverse of the card

Signature   Date

☐ I'd like to find out about giving a regular gift to BRF.

For help or advice regarding making a gift, please contact our fundraising team +44 (0)1235 462305

Your privacy

We will use your personal data to process this transaction. From time to time we may send you information about the work of BRF that we think may be of interest to you. Our privacy policy is available at **brf.org.uk/privacy**. Please contact us if you wish to discuss your mailing preferences.

Registered with

FUNDRAISING **REGULATOR**

↰ Please complete the other side of this form

Please return this form to 'Freepost BRF'
No other address information or stamp is needed

BRF

Bible Reading Fellowship is a charity (233280) and company limited by guarantee (301324), registered in England and Wales

GL0323

Guidelines forthcoming issue

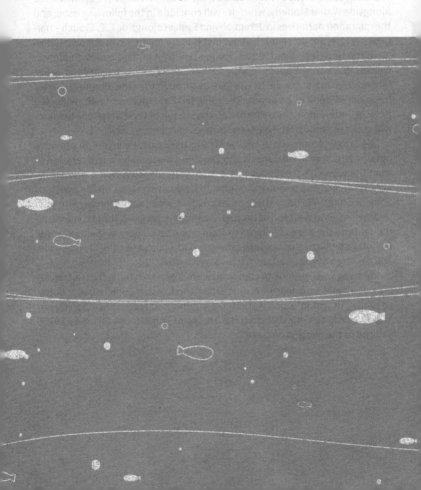

Guidelines forthcoming issue

The January–April 2024 issue of *Guidelines* is full of some real treats! I hope you are looking forward to it as much as we are.

We are delving into the many Old Testament books in this issue, with a host of wide-ranging topics. We'll be looking at book 3 of the Psalms alongside Bill Goodman, the third part of his five-part series; Daniel alongside Ernest Lucas, exploring the tensions between divine and human sovereignty; 1 Samuel 1—15 alongside Walter Moberly, which he will conclude in the following issue; and the migration narratives in Jeremiah and Ezekiel alongside C.L. Crouch – particularly relevant as we think about involuntary migration in our own times.

In the New Testament, David Spriggs will continue his series on biblical witness to John the Baptist, looking further at how John's ministry and Jesus' interweave. Joanna Collicutt will take us through the difficult and strangely fragmented book of 2 Corinthians, while Ian Paul tackles the oft-neglected book of Jude. Finally, as we head into the season of Lent, Stephen Finamore will guide us through the Easter narratives in John's gospel.

We also welcome some new writers to this issue. Evie Vernon provides notes on the women of Genesis and Exodus, a more imaginative series seen from the women's perspectives. We also welcome Ruth Wells, who brings her experience as a performance poet to bear with a series on the poetry of Song of Songs. We hope these more creative series will resonate with you. Meanwhile, Emma Ineson, bishop of Kensington, provides some challenging thoughts on the topic of failure. Far from being accusatory or guilt-inducing, Bishop Emma helps us see how failure is part of life, even the Christian life, and explores how we can learn to live well with it.

We hope you continue to enjoy and learn from everything that *Guidelines* provides. We love to hear what our readers think of particular issues or notes, so please do get in touch if you have anything to feed back – positive or negative! You can email **enquiries@brf.org.uk**, phone **+44 (0)1865 319700** or write to the address on page 2.

What the Bible means to me: Andy Angel

This reflection will make more sense if I tell you my story of engaging with the Bible. You see, my understanding of the authority of the Bible and its message come directly out of my reading of the Bible. Let me explain.

I grew up in a Christian household with both parents involved in ministry. The Bible was the word of God. I heard it read. I coloured in stories at Sunday school. I became a cathedral chorister and so had to get confirmed. Then, two godfathers gave me a Bible to celebrate this wonderful occasion. (I quite liked sneaking glasses of sherry afterwards with my mates.)

One of these Bibles had a plan to read the Bible in a year. So I did. Nobody asked me to do this. I did not tell my parents. But I read six chapters a day (four Old Testament, two New Testament) and was fascinated – particularly by the bits the ministers edited out of readings in churches and sermon series. They were the best bits. Suddenly the Bible became real for this teenager. Political intrigue, sex, violence, dysfunctional families, a generally errant people of God, frustration, exhaustion and crying out to God – this was just like real life for a preacher's kid whose dad worked in a theological college. And here I began to hear the voice of God speak among the all-too-human voices of the characters in the narratives I was reading. I grew to love the Bible as it made sense of life, and this somehow authenticated its being the word of God.

There is much more to my understanding of the authority of scripture now (which I cannot really offer you in 500 words) but the rootedness of God in human reality remains absolutely central. That God became human, living among us in Jesus and so eternally understanding what frail creatureliness means from the inside, remains central to my willingness to hear the over-arching story of scripture of a beautiful and rich creation, spoiled by human wrongdoing, but with a God who from Abraham onwards had a plan to put things right. My prayer life grew at the same time. Throughout my teens I would spend one or two hours a night in Bible reading and prayer. Clinical depression and cancer were in my immediate family so I had much to bring to God in prayer. The Psalms were incredibly helpful in teaching me that you can say anything to God – and pretty much anyhow. So the powerful mix of meeting the God I met in scripture in prayer as I read and often wrestled with scripture meant Bible reading was alive and real. It still is.

Recommended reading

The message of the kingdom of God: an ecology of equality and peace, and an economy of justice. Hope from beyond, sent to the present, is what Advent asks us to reckon with. Hope consists of God's jump leads sent from the future through time and space, wired right into our present pains, panics and predicaments. How can the light of Christ illuminate this present darkness?

An Advent Manifesto engages with two great Christmas hymns: the Magnificat and Benedictus. It is also rooted in poets, prophets and the theology and devotional writing of Howard Thurman, the black theologian and mentor to Martin Luther King Jr. Using the *lectio divina* approach to passages drawn from Isaiah and Luke, this book is an invitation to pray and practise that most ancient Advent prayer: 'Come, Lord Jesus, come.'

The following is an edited extract taken from the introduction.

This book was conceived at a time of enormous global turmoil. Government buildings in Washington DC had been stormed by supporters of Donald Trump. Black Lives Matter ferments with regular eruptions of protest. The world was gripped by a global pandemic that was seeing millions die. The European Union was squabbling over vaccines. Europe is at war for the first time in 70 years, with the very survival of Ukraine under threat. There are grain and gas shortages, which is driving up the cost of living. 'Food security' is now an issue, with a war pushing the price of fuel, food and fertiliser so high that nations are starving.

As though that was not enough to contend with, the politics of liberal democracies seem to be failing. Populism and extremism are becoming mainstream. Campaigns for equal rights – ethnicity, disability, sexuality and gender – are experiencing unprecedented pushback and encountering renewed hostility and oppression. In a world of turmoil and turbulence, there seems to be a decline in reason and responsibility, and ever-increasing privileging of unaccountable power and passionate intensity.

In the midst of this, refugees and asylum seekers are symptoms of wars, famines and political rights being denied in countries that were once progressive. Meanwhile, the church is beset with internal wrangling on sexuality, gender, declining numbers and collapses in revenue. There is a serious growing crisis of mental health among clergy, and a marked fragmentation in ecclesial systems of governance, with the institution experienced as increasingly irrelevant in the public sphere.

It is against this background that I thought I might try to write a book about the second coming of Christ. It is an Advent book, but also a reminder to me as much as it might be to any reader, that the life, work, focus, deeds and words of Jesus are about ushering in the kingdom of God, not propping up the church. Put another way, seek first the kingdom of God and God's righteousness and some of these other things may be added to you (Matthew 6:33). Matthew's beatitudes continue with a caveat for us to heed: 'For each day has enough worries of its own.' Quite so. We are called to abide in the uncertainty and trouble of life. There is no other life to live with.

Sometimes the church can seem to seek almost every available prop and lever of support it can, leaving the kingdom of God largely to itself and certainly forgetting about the righteousness of God. So we should not lose sight of our sin (it is within us, so not always easy to spot and call out, though others will see it). Our Advent must be framed in the context of the inexhaustible mercy and redemption of God.

God's love has consequences. As love arrived in the person of Jesus, unbidden and unmerited, so our love for others – especially 'the least' – must be unbidden too. Any love given is only ever unmerited, in the same way that none of us can earn or deserve God's love. So, we love because God first loved us (1 John 4). We didn't start this chain reaction. God is the originator. Love has come; it has arrived in Jesus. What will you return to God for this free, undeserved, infinite and inexhaustible gift?

This book is very much about the politics of paradise and consequences of God's love for us all. It takes as its cue one of the fundamental cores of liberation theology and many other kinds of liberation theologies, that all good religion worthy of the name of religion and faith is inherently political. If politics is about who gets what, when, where and how, the kingdom of God, if nothing else, is about precisely the same. The poor, the lame, the hungry, the marginalised and the stigmatised all receive God's kingdom first.

To order a copy of this book, please use the order form on page 151 or visit **brfonline.org.uk**.

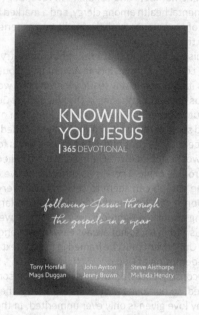

KNOWING
YOU, JESUS
| 365 DEVOTIONAL

*following Jesus through
the gospels in a year*

Tony Horsfall   John Ayrton   Steve Aisthorpe
Mags Duggan   Jenny Brown   Melinda Hendry

This 365-day devotional is a response to the famous prayer of Richard of Chichester 'to see thee more clearly, love thee more dearly and follow thee more nearly'. In it Tony Horsfall, Mags Duggan, John Ayrton, Jenny Brown, Steve Aisthorpe and Melinda Hendry present a detailed, chronological exploration of the life of Jesus of Nazareth, drawing from all four gospels. As we immerse ourselves in the gospel story, may we not only understand it better but experience transformation into the likeness of Christ our Saviour.

Knowing You, Jesus
Following Jesus through the gospels in a year
Tony Horsfall et al.
978 1 80039 185 7 £16.99
brfonline.org.uk

From the Community of Aidan and Hilda, here is a resource to create a daily rhythm of prayer, inspired by historic and contemporary Celtic Christian spirituality and earthed in the activities of everyday living. *Celtic Rhythms of Life* contains ready-to-use forms of prayer for morning, midday, evening and night, seven days a week. Each day also has its own theme, from resurrection on Sundays to the kingdom on Saturdays.

Celtic Rhythms of Life
Daily prayer from the Community of Aidan and Hilda
Graham Booth et al.
978 1 80039 229 8 £7.99 (pb) / £9.99 (hb)
brfonline.org.uk

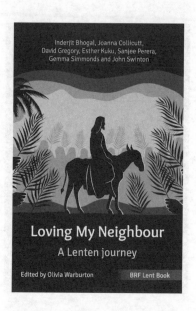

Inderjit Bhogal, Joanna Collicutt,
David Gregory, Esther Kuku, Sanjee Perera,
Gemma Simmonds and John Swinton

Loving My Neighbour
A Lenten journey

Edited by Olivia Warburton

BRF Lent Book

Loving My Neighbour takes us on a journey through the challenging terrain of how we can truly love one another, individually and in our communities. Daily Bible readings and reflections from Ash Wednesday to Easter Day explore how we can love in truth, love the vulnerable and the suffering, embrace difference, care for our world, and love ourselves as God loves us. Holy Week brings us back to reflect on Christ on the cross, who loved us to the very end.

Loving My Neighbour
A Lenten journey
Edited by Olivia Warburton
978 1 80039 215 1 £9.99
brfonline.org.uk

To order

Online: **brfonline.org.uk**
Telephone: **+44 (0)1865 319700**
Mon–Fri 9.30–17.00

Delivery times within the UK are normally 15 working days. Prices are correct at the time of going to press but may change without prior notice.

Title	Price	Qty	Total
An Advent Manifesto	£9.99		
Christmas Voices	£9.99		
Knowing You, Jesus	£16.99		
Celtic Rhythms of Life	£7.99 / £9.99		
Loving My Neighbour	£9.99		

POSTAGE AND PACKING CHARGES			
Order value	UK	Europe	Rest of world
Under £7.00	£2.00	Available on request	Available on request
£7.00–£29.99	£3.00		
£30.00 and over	FREE		

Total value of books	
Donation*	
Postage and packing	
Total for this order	

* Please complete and return the Gift Aid declaration on page 141.

Please complete in BLOCK CAPITALS

Title _____ First name/initials _____ Surname _____

Address _____

_____ Postcode _____

Acc. No. _____ Telephone _____

Email _____

Method of payment

☐ Cheque (made payable to BRF) ☐ MasterCard / Visa

Card no. ☐☐☐☐ ☐☐☐☐ ☐☐☐☐ ☐☐☐☐ ☐☐☐☐ ☐☐☐☐

Expires end ☐☐ ☐☐   Security code* ☐☐☐   * Last 3 digits on the reverse of the card

We will use your personal data to process this order. From time to time we may send you information about the work of BRF. Please contact us if you wish to discuss your mailing preferences **brf.org.uk/privacy**

Please return this form to:

BRF, 15 The Chambers, Vineyard, Abingdon OX14 3FE | **enquiries@brf.org.uk**

For terms and cancellation information, please visit **brfonline.org.uk/terms**.

Bible Reading Fellowship (BRF) is a charity (233280) and company limited by guarantee (301324), registered in England and Wales

BRF needs you!

If you're one of our regular *Guidelines* readers, you will know all about the rich rewards of regular Bible study and the value of serious daily notes to guide, inform and challenge you.

Here are some recent comments from *Guidelines* readers:

'… very thoughtful and spiritually helpful. [These notes] are speaking to the church as it is today, and therefore to Christians like us who live in today's world.'

'You have assembled an amazingly diverse group of people and their contributions are most certainly thoughtful.'

If you have similarly positive things to say about *Guidelines*, would you be willing to help spread the word about these valuable resources? One suggestion is to form a *Guidelines* reading group, not to take the place of private Bible study and prayer, but to give group members a chance to discover new dimensions and different interpretations as well as make new friends. It could be a breakfast or lunchtime meeting: short and to the point, or a more relaxed encounter, over a meal or a drink.

It doesn't need to be complicated: all *Guidelines* study notes have questions for reflection and suggestions for additional reading that lend themselves to group exploration.

We can supply further information if you need it and would love to hear about it if you do start a *Guidelines* reading group.

For more information:

- Email **enquiries@brf.org.uk**
- Telephone BRF on +44 (0)1865 319700 Mon–Fri 9.30–17.00
- Write to us at BRF, 15 The Chambers, Vineyard, Abingdon OX14 3FE

Enabling all ages to grow in faith

At BRF, we long for people of all ages to grow in faith and understanding of the Bible. That's what all our work as a charity is about.

- BRF's **Living Faith** ministry looks to see our founder Leslie Mannering's vision – to help people 'get a move on' spiritually – fulfilled in the 21st century. Our wide range of resources promotes Bible reading and prayer, our events bring people together to share this journey, and our Holy Habits initiative helps congregations grow in whole-life discipleship.

- We also want to make it easier for local churches to engage effectively in ministry and mission – by helping them bring new families into a growing relationship with God through **Messy Church** or by supporting churches as they nurture the spiritual life of older people through **Anna Chaplaincy**.

- Our **Parenting for Faith** team coaches parents and others to raise God-connected children and teens, and enables churches to fully support them.

Do you share our vision?

Though a significant proportion of BRF's funding is generated through our charitable activities, we are dependent on the generous support of individuals, churches and charitable trusts.

If you share our vision, would you help us to enable even more people of all ages to grow in faith? Your prayers and financial support are vital for the work that we do. You could:

- Support BRF's ministry with a regular donation;
- Support us with a one-off gift;
- Consider leaving a gift to BRF in your will (see page 154);
- Encourage your church to support BRF as part of your church's giving to home mission – perhaps focusing on a specific ministry or programme;
- Most important of all, support BRF with your prayers.

Donate at **brf.org.uk/donate** or use the form on pages 141–42.

Endings and beginnings

Therefore, if anyone is in Christ, the new creation has come: the old has gone, the new is here!
2 CORINTHIANS 5:17 (NIV)

This last quarter of the year is an interesting intersection of endings and beginnings. For many, September marks the start of a new school year, with all the challenges and opportunities that may bring. At the same time, we begin to see the end of the calendar year in sight. These beginnings and endings can be a useful time to reflect on the time past and the time to come.

For BRF's ministries, this time is a mixture of reflection and preparation. **Anna Chaplains** across the country are bringing fellowship and spiritual care to older people during this period where loneliness can be exacerbated. The **Living Faith** team are busy preparing resources to help people to explore their faith in the important seasons of Advent and, looking ahead, Lent. For **Messy Church**, this can be a busy quarter of the year, with many Messy Churches restarting after a summer break and planning ahead for the busy Christmas period. And our **Parenting for Faith** team are working to support parents and churches as many things change for children during this period.

While our work is constantly changing, we embrace the message of the Bible verse above – the old has gone, the new is here. We are excited for all the new ideas and projects we will be exploring in the months to come and we celebrate all that we have already accomplished in 2023.

Our vital work would not be possible without kind donations from individuals, charitable trusts and gifts in wills. If you would like to support BRF's work now and in the future you can become a Friend of BRF by making a monthly gift of £2 a month or more – we thank you for your friendship.

Find out more at **brf.org.uk/donate** or get in touch with us on **01235 462305** or via **giving@brf.org.uk**.

Judith Moore
Fundraising development officer

Give. Pray. Get involved.
brf.org.uk

GUIDELINES SUBSCRIPTION RATES

Please note our new subscription rates, current until 30 April 2024:

Individual subscriptions
covering 3 issues for under 5 copies, payable in advance
(including postage & packing):

	UK	Europe	Rest of world
Guidelines 1-year subscription	£19.05	£26.55	£30.45
Guidelines 3-year subscription (9 issues)	£54.45	N/A	N/A

Group subscriptions
covering 3 issues for 5 copies or more, sent to one UK address (post free):

Guidelines 1-year subscription £14.85 per set of 3 issues p.a.

Please note that the annual billing period for group subscriptions runs from 1 May to 30 April.

Overseas group subscription rates
Available on request. Please email **enquiries@brf.org.uk**.

Copies may also be obtained from Christian bookshops:

Guidelines £4.95 per copy

All our Bible reading notes can be ordered online
by visiting **brfonline.org.uk/subscriptions**

GUIDELINES

Guidelines is also available as
an app for Android, iPhone and iPad
brfonline.org.uk/apps

All our Bible reading notes can be ordered online by visiting
brfonline.org.uk/subscriptions

Title _____ First name/initials _____ Surname _____

Address _____

_____ Postcode _____

Telephone _____ Email _____

Please send *Guidelines* beginning with the January 2024 / May 2024 /
September 2024 issue (*delete as appropriate*):

(*please tick box*)

	UK	Europe	Rest of world
Guidelines 1-year subscription	☐ £19.05	☐ £26.55	☐ £30.45
Guidelines 3-year subscription	☐ £54.45	N/A	N/A

Optional donation to support the work of BRF £ _____

Total enclosed £ _____ (cheques should be made payable to 'BRF')

Please complete and return the Gift Aid declaration on page 143 to make your
donation even more valuable to us.

Please charge my MasterCard / Visa with £ _____

Card no. ☐☐☐☐ ☐☐☐☐ ☐☐☐☐ ☐☐☐☐

Expires end ☐☐ ☐☐ Security code ☐☐☐ Last 3 digits on the reverse of the card

To set up a Direct Debit, please complete the Direct Debit instruction on page 159.

We will use your personal data to process this order. From time to time we may send you
information about the work of BRF. Please contact us if you wish to discuss your mailing
preferences **brf.org.uk/privacy**

Please return this form with the appropriate payment to:
BRF, 15 The Chambers, Vineyard, Abingdon OX14 3FE

For terms and cancellation information, please visit **brfonline.org.uk/terms**.

Bible Reading Fellowship is a charity (233280) and company limited by guarantee (301324),
registered in England and Wales

GUIDELINES GIFT SUBSCRIPTION FORM

☐ I would like to give a gift subscription (please provide both names and addresses):

Title .... First name/initials .... Surname ....

Address ....

.... Postcode ....

Telephone .... Email ....

Gift subscription name ....

Gift subscription address ---

.... Postcode ....

Gift message (20 words max. or include your own gift card):

....

....

Please send *Guidelines* beginning with the January 2024 / May 2024 /
September 2024 issue *(delete as appropriate)*:

(please tick box)	UK	Europe	Rest of world
Guidelines 1-year subscription	☐ £19.05	☐ £26.55	☐ £30.45
Guidelines 3-year subscription	☐ £54.45	N/A	N/A

Optional donation to support the work of BRF £ ....

Total enclosed £ .... (cheques should be made payable to 'BRF')

Please complete and return the Gift Aid declaration on page 143 to make your
donation even more valuable to us.

Please charge my MasterCard / Visa with £ ....

Card no. ☐☐☐☐ ☐☐☐☐ ☐☐☐☐ ☐☐☐☐

Expires end ☐☐ ☐☐ M M Y Y   Security code ☐☐☐   Last 3 digits on the
reverse of the card

To set up a Direct Debit, please complete the Direct Debit instruction on page 159.

We will use your personal data to process this order. From time to time we may send you
information about the work of BRF. Please contact us if you wish to discuss your mailing
preferences **brf.org.uk/privacy**

Please return this form with the appropriate payment to:
BRF, 15 The Chambers, Vineyard, Abingdon OX14 3FE

For terms and cancellation information, please visit **brfonline.org.uk/terms**.

Bible Reading Fellowship is a charity (233280) and company limited by guarantee (301324),
registered in England and Wales

You can pay for your annual subscription to our Bible reading notes using Direct Debit. You need only give your bank details once, and the payment is made automatically every year until you cancel it. If you would like to pay by Direct Debit, please use the form opposite, entering your BRF account number under 'Reference number'.

You are fully covered by the Direct Debit Guarantee:

The Direct Debit Guarantee

- This Guarantee is offered by all banks and building societies that accept instructions to pay Direct Debits.
- If there are any changes to the amount, date or frequency of your Direct Debit, Bible Reading Fellowship will notify you 10 working days in advance of your account being debited or as otherwise agreed. If you request Bible Reading Fellowship to collect a payment, confirmation of the amount and date will be given to you at the time of the request.
- If an error is made in the payment of your Direct Debit, by Bible Reading Fellowship or your bank or building society, you are entitled to a full and immediate refund of the amount paid from your bank or building society.
- If you receive a refund you are not entitled to, you must pay it back when Bible Reading Fellowship asks you to.
- You can cancel a Direct Debit at any time by simply contacting your bank or building society. Written confirmation may be required. Please also notify us.

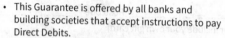

Instruction to your bank or building society to pay by Direct Debit

Please fill in the whole form using a ballpoint pen and return with order form to:
BRF, 15 The Chambers, Vineyard, Abingdon OX14 3FE

Service User Number: | 5 | 5 | 8 | 2 | 2 | 9 |

Name and full postal address of your bank or building society

To: The Manager | Bank/Building Society

Address

Postcode

Name(s) of account holder(s)

Branch sort code

Bank/Building Society account number

Reference number

Instruction to your Bank/Building Society
Please pay Bible Reading Fellowship Direct Debits from the account detailed
in this instruction, subject to the safeguards assured by the Direct Debit Guarantee.
I understand that this instruction may remain with Bible Reading Fellowship
and, if so, details will be passed electronically to my bank/building society.

Signature(s)

Banks and Building Societies may not accept Direct Debit instructions for some
types of account.

Enabling all ages to grow in faith

Anna Chaplaincy
Living Faith
Messy Church
Parenting for Faith

BRF is a Christian charity that resources individuals and churches. Our vision is to enable people of all ages to grow in faith and understanding of the Bible and to see more people equipped to exercise their gifts in leadership and ministry.

To find out more about our work, visit
brf.org.uk